HTML

HTML code is a programming language used in website building and website templates. It is used to format the look and format of a web page, to set design features such as basic layout, colors, and fonts. *HTML: The Ultimate Guide* provides a crash course in HTML, its history, key features, different versions available, various tags and elements, as well as the advantages and disadvantages.

This book also covers the fundamental concepts of CSS and JavaScript and guides the reader through creating websites and games with it. As the reader progresses through the lessons, they will learn how to insert JavaScript commands directly into the HTML document, and how the script executes when viewed in browser.

This is a valuable resource for anyone who wants to create a website or any 2d and 3d game in HTML. After finishing this book, readers will be able to quickly build their website or game with absolute ease.

This book is organized as follows:

- Discusses code optimization in HTML code, Web Scripting and Security ideas in HTML.

- Introduces the HTML for Game Development, benefits and types of games (2d and 3d).

- Includes a Cheat Sheet of HTML where you will get all key terms and useful information that is easy to access.

HTML
The Ultimate Guide

Sufyan bin Uzayr

CRC Press
Taylor & Francis Group
Boca Raton London New York

CRC Press is an imprint of the
Taylor & Francis Group, an **informa** business

First edition published 2024
by CRC Press
2385 Executive Center Drive, Suite 320, Boca Raton, FL 33431

and by CRC Press
4 Park Square, Milton Park, Abingdon, Oxon, OX14 4RN

CRC Press is an imprint of Taylor & Francis Group, LLC

© 2024 Sufyan bin Uzayr

Library of Congress Cataloging-in-Publication Data

Names: Bin Uzayr, Sufyan, author.
Title: HTML : the ultimate guide / Sufyan Bin Uzayr.
Description: First edition. | Boca Raton : CRC Press, 2023. | Includes
bibliographical references.
Identifiers: LCCN 2023003120 (print) | LCCN 2023003121 (ebook) | ISBN
9781032413259 (paperback) | ISBN 9781032413266 (hardback) | ISBN
9781003357537 (ebook)
Subjects: LCSH: HTML (Document markup language)--Amateurs' manuals.
Classification: LCC QA76.76.H94 B56 2023 (print) | LCC QA76.76.H94
(ebook) | DDC 005.7/2--dc23/eng/20230310
LC record available at https://lccn.loc.gov/2023003120
LC ebook record available at https://lccn.loc.gov/2023003121

ISBN: 9781032413266 (hbk)
ISBN: 9781032413259 (pbk)
ISBN: 9781003357537 (ebk)

DOI: 10.1201/9781003357537

Typeset in Minion
by KnowledgeWorks Global Ltd.

For Dad

Contents

About the Author

Sufyan bin Uzayr is a writer, coder, and entrepreneur with more than a decade of experience in the industry. He has authored several books in the past, pertaining to a diverse range of topics, ranging from History to Computers/IT.

Sufyan is the Director of Parakozm, a multinational IT company specializing in EdTech solutions. He also runs Zeba Academy, an online learning and teaching vertical with a focus on STEM fields.

Sufyan specializes in a wide variety of technologies such as JavaScript, Dart, WordPress, Drupal, Linux, and Python. He holds multiple degrees, including ones in Management, IT, Literature, and Political Science.

Sufyan is a digital nomad, dividing his time between four countries. He has lived and taught in universities and educational institutions around the globe. Sufyan takes a keen interest in technology, politics, literature, history, and sports, and in his spare time, he enjoys teaching coding and English to young students. Learn more at sufyanism.com

Acknowledgments

There are many people who deserve being on this page because this book would not have come into existence without their support. That said, some names deserve a special mention, and I am genuinely grateful to:

- My parents, for everything they have done for me.

- My siblings, for helping with things back home.

- The Parakozm team, especially Divya Sachdeva, Jaskiran Kaur, and Vartika, for offering great amounts of help and assistance during the book-writing process.

- The CRC team, especially Sean Connelly and Danielle Zarfati, for ensuring that the book's content, layout, formatting, and everything else remain perfect throughout.

- Reviewers of this book, for going through the manuscript and providing their insight and feedback.

- Typesetters, cover designers, printers, and everyone else, for their part in the development of this book.

- All the folks associated with Zeba Academy, either directly or indirectly, for their help and support.

- The programming community, in general, and the web development community, in particular, for all their hard work and efforts.

Sufyan bin Uzayr

CHAPTER 1

Crash Course HTML

IN THIS CHAPTER

> ➤ Frontend vs. Backend

> ➤ HTML

> ➤ Tags and Elements

This HyperText Markup Language (HTML) book is for complete beginners, so it's written in a simple way so that beginners do not get confused. We have also provided an example for each topic and concept with proper details of correct code output and legitimate HTML code.

By the end of this HTML book, we are sure you will be good in HTML and start creating your own website structures. However, you need to learn some other languages like Cascading Style Sheet (CSS) and JavaScript to create an attractive and beautiful website. All these languages are also known as frontend languages.

Before getting deeper into HTML, first we will discuss what is frontend technology and backend technology. We will also discuss under which categories the various technology fall off.

FRONTEND VS. BACKEND

The frontend of a website is everything that can be viewed and interacted with through a browser.[1] Therefore, creating this visual part is called frontend development. The designer who creates the user interface and plans

DOI: 10.1201/9781003357537-1

the experience is also a frontend developer because they collaborate on the same part of the project.

To create the frontend, the engineer used a combination of HTML (used for basic page structure and content), CSS (used for visual editing), and JavaScript (to make the website interactive). The same tools are used to create Progressive Web Apps (mobile apps that look like native apps but are built using frontend technologies). To be a good frontend developer, you need to focus on the following list of technology:

- HTML
- CSS
- Bootstrap
- JavaScript
- React
- React Native
- Angular
- Flutter
- NPM
- Vue.js
- Ionic

The backend, on the other hand, is everything that goes on behind the scenes. It contains the server that hosts your web pages and the underlying logic that manages your website's functionality and processes. There is a detailed explanation of the inner workings of the web application if you want to take a look. Backends are built using a variety of technologies such as Java, PHP, Ruby, C#, Django, frameworks for various other languages, and sometimes JavaScript.

MOSTLY USED FRONTEND TECHNOLOGY

The basic toolset of the frontend is well-defined: HTML, CSS, and JavaScript. However, frontend development technologies can be extended with package managers, CSS preprocessors, frameworks, etc. HTML is the primary frontend technology here.

HTML is a language for building websites. This language is commonly used to structure web documents. You can define elements such as headings and paragraphs and embed images, videos, and other media.

How Does HTML Work as Frontend?

HTML contains a set of shortcodes called tags that are normalized into text files by website builders.[2] The text is saved as an HTML (.html) file and can be viewed in any browser.

Hypertext is a way of navigating the Internet by clicking hyperlinks (specific text that takes you to another page). Hyper means nonlinear, it has no predefined order, so it can be moved elsewhere. Markup determines the properties to apply to text containing HTML tags. A tag identifies it as a particular type of text. As a language, it contains syntax like any other language.

The top is the HTML5 document type declaration is to be done. If not included, different browsers will render it in their own way. The text between and specifies the web page, and the text between and determines the displayed content.

Next Is CSS

CSS is a stylesheet language. Applied to define how HTML elements are rendered on a web page in terms of design, layout, and variations for different devices with different screen sizes. CSS handles the layout of many different websites simultaneously.

How CSS Work as Frontend Technology?

CSS interacts with HTML elements, which are the components of web pages.[3] CSS uses selectors to communicate with HTML. A selector is a piece of CSS code that defines the portion of HTML that a CSS style affects. Its declaration contains properties and values used by the selector. The properties define font size, color, and margins. The values are the settings for those properties.

CSS is written in plain text using any text editor or word processor. If you want to explore how CSS code is implemented in HTML content, you have three options: Instead of adding an extra instance of CSS code to each HTML element that needs to be changed. To use an external stylesheet, the .html file must contain a header section that links to the external stylesheet. Internal stylesheets are CSS directives that are inserted directly into the header of a given .html page. Inline styles are CSS snippets included within the HTML code itself.

We also have CSS framework with us; you can use them to make your workflow more flexible. A CSS framework is a set of standard CSS and HTML files. CSS frameworks not only help create responsive designs, but they also offer a variety of symmetrical layouts that save developers the hassle of writing code from scratch for every occasion. These are considered good choices for different platforms and screen sizes. With the user interface components, grid systems, layouts, also many other features, CSS frameworks greatly speed up your development workflow. There are many frameworks in CSS Universe such as Bootstrap, Foundation, Semantic UI, Materialize, Material Design Lite, and Lightweight (Pure).

DOM: THE STRUCTURE OF WEBSITES

The Document Object Model (DOM) is defined as a programming interface for HTML and XML documents.[4] Interpret the page so that the program can change the structure, style, and content of the document. The DOM renders documents as nodes and objects and allows programming languages to connect them to the page.

How DOM Works

A web page is a document that can be viewed in a browser window or in HTML source code. The DOM represents the document in a modifiable way. It is an object-oriented representation of web pages that can be modified using a scripting language such as JavaScript.

DOM must resemble with World Wide Web Consortium (W3C) and WHATWG standards to work in the latest modern browsers. A modern DOM is built using multiple APIs that work together. The DOM Core specifies the objects that fully describe and contain the document.

The DOM currently consists of two parts such as DOM Core and DOM HTML. The DOM Core represents the functionality used for XML documents and serves as the basis for DOM HTML. All DOM implementations MUST support the interfaces listed as "basic" in the core specification. In addition, XML implementations MUST support interfaces listed as "extensions" in the core specification. The Level 1 DOM HTML specification defines additional features required for HTML documents.

Where DOM Came From

The DOM was built as a specification to make JavaScript scripts and Java programs portable across various Web browsers.[5] The Dynamic HTML is the ancestor of the DOM and was originally viewed primarily in browsers. The DOM was influenced by the SGML Groves and HyTime standards.

JavaScript

JavaScript (JS) is the most popular scripting language.[6] This language is best known for providing both frontend and backend development. It is applied to make web pages dynamic.

How JavaScript Works

JS enhances the overall interactivity of your website. You can model animated UI components such as image sliders, popups, and rich website navigation menus. JavaScript provides advanced functionality to websites that HTML and CSS alone cannot achieve. JavaScript allows web pages to dynamically update in response to user actions. As like Bootstrap, JS also has various libraries and frameworks. Now let's define what constitutes a JS framework, what a JS library is, and what purpose they serve.

Library and Framework

A framework is a template for building a website or web application. They provide a structure on which the entire project can be placed. Once the framework determines the page template, it builds a structure with specific areas allocated to embed the framework code.

Libraries are sets of pre-built code snippets that are used and reused to implement core JavaScript functionality. Snippets can be easily integrated into existing project code as needed. As such, a library is a specialized tool for a particular coding need, not a general-purpose machine for maintaining entire existing projects.

JavaScript AS BACKEND

JavaScript as an end-to-end development environment, we have to mention its backend implementation. JavaScript is so popular that the world of software engineering has adapted JS to the backend specification. Node.js is the most popular tool for web server-side development using JavaScript. However, it is neither a framework nor a library. Basically, it is a runtime environment based on Chrome's V8 JavaScript engine. Now come back on this chapter which is totally based on HTML Crash course. We will cover every topic of it so that beginners can understand each and every step of theory as well as practical.

Now let's see what a markup language is and why it is considered a markup language. Next, explore other markup languages available to software engineers today.

WHAT IS A MARKUP LANGUAGE?

A markup language is a language that text that computer can manipulate it. Most markup languages are human-readable because annotations are written in a way that distinguishes them from the text itself. For example, in HTML, XML, and XHTML, the markup tags are < and >. Text contained within any of these characters is considered part of the markup language.

The latest version of HTML5 is now widely adopted by developers and is used by about 90% of websites. Do not confuse the two terms. HTML and HTML5 are one and the same, but HTML introduced new features to the most popular markup language.

HTML – HYPERTEXT MARKUP LANGUAGE

HTML is used as a basic language of the web and the most common language you use as a web designer or developer.[7] In fact, it may be the markup language you use at work.

All web pages are written in the HTML variant. HTML defines how images, multimedia, and text are displayed in web browsers. This language contains elements for connecting documents (hypertext) and making web documents interactive (such as forms). Many people refer to HTML as "website code", but it's really just a markup language. Neither term is strictly wrong. I hear people, including web professionals, using the two terms interchangeably.

HTML is a predefined standard markup language. It is based on Standard Generalized Markup Language (SGML). It is a language that only uses tags to define the simple structure of text. The elements and tags are defined by the < and > characters.

HTML is the most famous markup language on the web today, but it's not the only option for web development. As HTML developed, it became more and more complex, combining style and content tags into one language. Finally, the W3C has decided that a Web page's style and content should be separated. Tags that only define content remain in HTML, while tags that define style are deprecated in favor of CSS.

When you create an HTML page, the markup is never displayed to the user. When you open the site, you will see related text, images, and videos.

But HTML pulls the strings behind all this. This will let all browsers know how to organize things. HTML allows you to group paragraphs, headings, images, videos, and more. You can create complex forms to display information exactly the way you want it.

Although HTML is not a markup language, 94% of websites use HTML as their markup language, making it the most popular. Its ease of use has made it the markup language of the web, but there are many different markup languages, each with different uses.

HTML is generally much more forgiving than other markup languages such as XML. It is case insensitive and will compile even if you omit the end tag. For decades, HTML has been an easy-to-use starting point for people learning web development. It also works well with frameworks such as CSS and Bootstrap. As already mentioned, markup languages define how electronic documents are interpreted.

HTML INTRODUCTION

HTML is the standard markup language for documents viewed in Web browsers.[8] It can help through technologies such as CSS and scripting languages such as JavaScript. The Web browser receives various HTML documents from a Web server or local storage and transforms the documents into multimedia Web pages. HTML semantically defines the structure of web pages and originally contained guidelines for the appearance of documents.

HTML elements are the building blocks of HTML pages. You can use HTML constructs to insert other objects such as images and interactive forms into the rendered page. HTML provides a better way to create structured documents by marking up the structural semantics of text such as: text formatting, tables, headings, paragraphs, lists, links, quotes, and other elements. HTML elements are delimited by tags written in curly braces. Tags such as <body> places content directly on the web page. Other tags, such <head>, provide information about the body of the document and can contain other tags as sub elements. Browsers do not display HTML tags but use them to interpret page content. The Hypertext is text displayed on a system that contains links to other text that the user can immediately access, usually by clicking a mouse or pressing a key. In addition to text, hypertext can include tables, lists, forms, images, and other presentation elements. It is an easy-to-use and flexible format for exchanging information over the Internet.

The markup uses a series of markup tags to characterize text elements in a document and tell the web browser what the document should look like. HTML was first developed in 1990 by a physicist, Tim Berners-Lee. He is considered the father of the Internet. However, in 1996, the W3C became the body controlling the HTML specifications. HTML became an international standard (ISO) in 2000. HTML5 is now the latest version of HTML. It offers a faster and more robust approach to web development.

HTML can embed programs written in various scripting languages, such as JavaScript, to affect the behavior and content of web pages. CSS embedding defines the appearance and layout of content. The W3C, the former maintainer of HTML and now the maintainer of CSS standards, has supported the use of CSS in explicit presentation HTML since 1997. A form of HTML, called version HTML5, is used to create video and audio using the <canvas> element, together with JavaScript.

HISTORY

The first version was written by Tim Berners-Lee in 1993. Since then, there have been various versions of HTML.[9] The most widely used version in the 2000s was HTML 4, which became the official standard in December 1999.

Another version, XHTML, is HTML rewritten as XML. This is the standard markup language used to create other markup languages. Hundreds of XML languages include GML, MathML, MusicML, and RSS. Each of these languages is written in a common language (XML), so its content can be easily shared between applications. XML has such powerful potential that it's no surprise that the W3C created his XML version of HTML called XHTML. It became an official standard in 2000 and was updated in 2002. It's very similar to HTML, but with some stricter rules. Sometimes you want strict rules for all XML languages. Without it, interoperability between applications would be impossible.

Most pages on the web are built with 4.01 or XHTML 1.0. However, in recent years, the W3C has been working on a new version of HTML, HTML5.

HTML is a markup language that browsers use to assemble text, images, and other material into visual or audio web pages.[10] Default properties for each HTML tag element are defined by the browser. These properties can be modified or extended using more of her CSS from the website designer.

The 1988 Technical Report ISO TR 9537 Techniques for using SGML contains many text elements. These formatting commands are derived from commands used by typesetters to manually format documents.

Here below there are many types of content that can be added to web pages using other versions of HTML. The early HTML was very simple, but new versions have been released with more features. However, if web designers want to add content or functionality not supported by HTML, they must do so using nonstandard proprietary technologies such as those of Adobe. These technologies require users to install their browser plug-ins, which in some cases may prevent some users from accessing content. HTML5 adds support for many new features that allow you to get more out of HTML without relying on nonstandard, proprietary technologies.

Type of HTML Content	HTML 1.2	HTML 4.01	HTML5	Purpose
Heading	Yes	Yes	Yes	It is used to organize page content by adding headings and subheadings to the top of each section of the page
Paragraph	Yes	Yes	Yes	It identifies the paragraphs of text
Address that contains contact information	Yes	Yes	Yes	It identifies a block of text
Anchor	Yes	Yes	Yes	It links to other web content
List	Yes	Yes	Yes	It organizes items into a list
Image	Yes	Yes	Yes	It is used to embed a photograph or drawing into a web page
Table	No	Yes	Yes	It organizes data into rows and columns
Style	No	Yes	Yes	It adds CSS to control how objects on a web page are presented
Script	No	Yes	Yes	It adds JavaScript to make pages respond to user behaviors (more interactive)
Audio	No	No	Yes	It adds audio to a web page with a single tag
Video	No	No	Yes	It adds video to a web page with a single tag
Canvas	No	No	Yes	It adds an invisible drawing pad to a web page, on which you can add drawings using JavaScript

HTML FUTURE

HTML has come a long way. It has gone from the simple idea of sharing documents between different computers to being part of almost everything we do on the Internet.

HTML has changed with the world with new requirements and technologies. It's also constantly changing and adding new features. A recent update to HTML5 added canvas. This was really great. You can use the canvas to draw shapes, images, text, animations, and even entire games.

As technology becomes more complex to meet the growing demand for more reliable devices, the future of HTML is its adaptability to change, operability across devices, and developer and user interaction.

HTML VERSIONS

Let's take a quick look to the list of different versions of HTML and a timeline of their features:[11]

- 1991 – Tim Berners-Lee created HTML 1.0.

- 1993 – Its 1.0 version was first released in 1993. This version had only basic features. This version also didn't allow tags such as text tables and fonts.

- Nov 24, 1995 – HTML 2.0 was released by the end of this year. All features of HTML 1.0 have been carried over to HTML 2.0 and new features have been added. Until HTML 3.0 is released, it will remain the standard markup language for building websites.

- January 14, 1997:

  - HTML 3.2 was published as W3C Recommendation.

  - In 1997, the first version of HTML was developed by W3C.

  - Form elements were properly supported in this version. One of the most significant additions in this release is support to CSS in the pages.

- 1999:

  - HTML 4.01 was published as a W3C Recommendation on December 14, 1999. This version was the most successful of all the previous HTML versions.

  - This release adds features such as improved multimedia, scripting, and printing capabilities.

DIFFERENT VERSIONS OF HTML

HTML has never been the way it is right now.[12] HTML, like many languages, has evolved over time and is much better and more versatile today than it was a long time ago. Different versions of HTML have different properties. But today we use HTML5, which is the latest version of HTML.

- HTML 1.0 (released in 1991)

- HTML 2.0 (released in 1995)

- HTML 3.2 (released in 1997)

- HTML 4.01 (released in 1999)

- XHTML (released in 2000)

- HTML5 (released in 2014)

1. **HTML 1.0:** It was the basic version of HTML with less support for a wide range of HTML elements. It does not have rich features such as styling and other things related to how content will be rendered in a browser. This initial version doesn't provide support for tables, font support, etc.

2. **HTML 2:** It was developed in 1995 to improve HTML version 1.0. It was developed to maintain common rules and regulations across different browsers. It improves a lot in terms of marker marks. In version 2.0, the concept of form came into effect. Forms were developed but still had basic markups like text boxes, buttons, etc.

   Also, the table came as an HTML tag. Now, in version 2.0, browsers also came up with the concept of creating custom markup layers that were specific to the browser itself. The main intention of the W3C is to maintain standards across different web browsers so that those browsers understand and render HTML tags in a similar way.

3. **HTML 3.2:** HTML 3.2 was published by W3C Recommendation. It was the very first version developed exclusively by the W3C. With HTML 3.2, HTML tags were further improved. It had many new features like tables, superscript, subscript, etc. The two most important features introduced in it were tables and text flow around images.

   Now it has better support for the new form of elements. Another important feature it implemented was CSS support. It is CSS that provides functions that will make HTML tags look better when rendered in browsers. CSS helps style HTML elements.

After browsers were upgraded to it, the browser also supported frame tags, although the HTML specification still does not support iframe tags. Tables were widely used and are still used by programmers, but it is no longer recommended. In HTML5, div tags and other semantic elements are more often used instead of the table element.

4. **HTML 4.01:** It is expanded support for CSS. In version 3.2, CSS was embedded into the HTML page itself. So if a website has different web pages to apply the style of each page, we need to put CSS on each web page. So there was a repetition of the same CSS block.

   To overcome this, the concept of an external stylesheet appeared in version 4.01. Under this concept, an external CSS file could be developed and this external style file could be included in the HTML itself. HTML 4.01 provided support for additional new HTML tags.

   HTML 4.01 was a revised version of HTML 4.0; it also included features for people with disabilities to improve their interactivity with the global world through the Internet.

5. **XHTML:** XHTML is called Extensible Hypertext Markup Language.[13] It can consider as a part of the XML markup language because it has features of both XML and HTML. It is extended from XML and HTML. It can be considered as a better version of HTML. XHTML version:

   • XHTML is a different language that began as a reformulation of HTML 4.01 using XML 1.0. Now it is no longer being developed as a stand-alone standard.

   • XHTML version 1.0 was published as a W3C Recommendation on January 26, 2000, later revised and republished on August 1, 2002.

   • XHTML 1.1 was published on May 31, 2001, as W3C Recommendation. It is based on the XHTML 1.0 Strict, but with minor changes, it can be adapted.

   • XHTML 2.0 was abandoned in 2009 in favor of work on HTML5 and XHTML5. XHTML 2.0 was now incompatible with XHTML 1.x.

6. **HTML5:** HTML5 is the best version of HTML to date. HTML5 has improved user interactivity so much and also reduced the load on the device.

HTML5 fully supports all kinds of media applications out there. HTML5 supports both audio and video media content. HTML5 also provides full support for running JavaScript in the background.

MARKUP IN HTML

HTML markup consists of various key components, including those called tags (their attributes), character-based data types, character references, and entity references. HTML tags are most often found in pairs such as <h1> and </h1>, although some represent empty elements and are therefore unpaired, such as <img>. The first tag is a pair is the start tag and the second is the end tag (also called opening tags and ending tags).

Another important part is the HTML document type declaration that triggers standard mode rendering.

The following is an example of the program given below.

```
<!DOCTYPE html>
<html>
  <head>
    <title> Document Title </title>
  </head>
  <body>
    <div>
        <h1> Simple Example of Markup in HTML </h1>
        <p> You are learning HTML! </p>
    </div>
  </body>
</html>
```

The output of the code is given below.

Simple Example of Markup in HTML

You are learning HTML!

HTML Markup.

The text between <html> and </html> describes the web page; the text between <body> and </body> is the visible content of the page. The

<title> This is a title</title> tag defines the browser page title displayed on browser tabs and window titles, and the <div> tag defines page divisions used for easy styling. A <meta> element can be used between <head> and </head> to define a web page's metadata. The <!DOCTYPE html> document type declaration is for HTML5. If the declaration is not included, various browsers fall back into "quirks mode" for rendering.

Where HyperText is the method by which Internet users navigate the web. By clicking on text called hyperlinks, then users are brought to new pages. The use of hyper means it is not linear so users can go anywhere on the Internet just by clicking on the available links. Markup is what HTML tags do to the text inside them; then mark it as a specific type of text. For example, markup text comes in the form of boldface or italicized type to draw specific attention to a word or phrase.

BASIC HTML CONCEPTS

Structure of an HTML Document

The <!DOCTYPE html> declaration specifies the version of HTML used in the document.[14] Every HTML document must start with this declaration so that browsers can render the page in accordance with HTML standards.

There are several <!DOCTYPE> types defined for each version of HTML. <!DOCTYPE> – The doctype declaration indicates the type of document and version of HTML used on the web page. Each version has a different doctype declaration. This example uses the HTML5 Doctype.

```
<!DOCTYPE>
```

All contents on a web page are written between <html> and </html> tags. The <html> element is used to tell browsers that this is an HTML document. <html> – It is the root tag of the document that describes the entire web page. It is also paired tag, i.e. it also has a closing </html> tag. Everything will be written inside these tags.

```
<html>
//rest of the code
</html>
```

The <head> element contains metadata (that is data about the HTML document), character set, document name, styles, etc. This data is not displayed to viewers. This tag contains information about the document, such as its title, author information, web page description, and so on. It has various tags to perform these functions. It is also called a couple tag.

```
<head>
  . . rest of the code
  </head>
```

The <title> shows the title of the website in the browser tab when the page is loaded. It is written between <title> and </title> tags.

```
<title>
  . . rest of the code
  </title>
```

The <body> tag contains the content of the web page (i.e. text, images, videos, etc.). Content is written between <body> and </body>. The body tag contains all information that will be displayed on the web page. If you want anything to appear on the page, you must write it in these tags.

```
<body>
  . . rest of the code
</body>
```

Heading elements contain different types of headings. There are six heading levels – <h1> – <h6>, where <h1> is the most important and <h6> least important tags.

```
<h1> </h1>
<h2> </h2>
<h3> </h3>
<h4> </h4>
<h5> </h5>
<h6> </h6>
```

The <p> element contains paragraphs of the text. The content is written between <p> and </p> tags.

```
<p> </p>
```

Example:

```
<!DOCTYPE HTML>
<html>
  <head>
```

```
    <meta HTTP-equiv="Content-Type" content="text/
HTML; charset=utf-8">
    <title>Title of the document</title>
    <style>
    body{
      width:500px;
      margin:0 auto,
    }
    </style>
  </head>

  <body>
    <h1>
      Structure of an HTML Document
    </h1>
    <h2> Aenean placerat commodo tortor at ornare.
Suspendisse et rutrum eros. In quis velit nunc.
Fusce auctor felis id tellus euismod aliquam.
Pellentesque habitant morbi senectus et netus et
malesuada fames ac turpis egestas.
    </h2>
    <p>Donec vitae pharetra nisl. Nulla consequat,
purus semper viverra congue, risus ex bibendum
urna, nec fringilla mi ipsum in mauris. Curabitur
id bibendum arcu, id efficitur risus. </p>
    <h2> Nulla consequat, purus semper viverra
congue, risus ex bibendum urna, nec  </h2>
  </body>
</html>
```

HTML DOCUMENT TYPE

All HTML documents must begin with a <!DOCTYPE> declaration. A declaration is not an HTML tag. It is "information" to the browser about what type of document to expect.

In HTML5, the <!DOCTYPE> declaration is simple. The <!DOCTYPE> declaration is NOT case-sensitive.

- <!DOCTYPE html>

- <!DocType html>

- <!Doctype html>

- <!doctype html>

Example:

```
<!DOCTYPE html>
<html lang="en">
<head>
    <meta charset="UTF-8">
    <meta HTTP-equiv="X-UA-Compatible"
content="IE=edge">
    <meta name="viewport" content="width=device-
width, initial-scale=1.0">
    <title>Document</title>
</head>
<body>
    <h1> Doctype of HTML </h1>
    <code> &lt;!DOCTYPE html&gt; </code> <br>
    <code> &lt;!DocType html&gt; </code> <br>
    <code> &lt;!Doctype html&gt; </code> <br>
    <code> &lt;!doctype html&gt; </code> <br>
    </body>
</html>
```

The output of the code is given below.

Doctype of HTML

```
<!DOCTYPE html>
<!DocType html>
<!Doctype html>
<!doctype html>
```

HTML Doctype.

There are some basic HTML concepts such as elements, tags, and attributes.[15] Elements are a main structural unit of a web page. The tags are used to define HTML elements, and attributes provide additional information about these elements.

HTML TAGS

Basically, tags are used to structure website content (text, hyperlinks, images, media, etc.).[16] These are not displayed in browsers; they only "instruct" browsers how to display the content of the web page.

There are over hundreds of tags and you can find them in any other HTML lesson. These tags are written in curly brackets (e.g. <html>). Most HTML tags come in pairs, such as <p> – </p> tags. The first tag in the pair is called the start (opening) tag and the second tag is the end (closing) tag. The information is written between the opening and closing tags. However, there are unpaired or empty tags that only have a start tag (e.g. <img/>).

A document is created using different types of tags. HTML tags can be defined and divided on a different basis. Let's take a look at them in the following sections of this chapter. We have divided these tags based on the following classifications:

- Paired and Unpaired Tags

- Self-Closing Tags

- Utility-Based Tags

Let's explain the following are the paired and unpaired tags in HTML in detail with the help of examples.

Paired Tag

A tag is known as a paired tag if the tag consists of a start tag and an end tag as a companion tag. An HTML paired tag begins with an opening tag: the name of the tag enclosed in curly brackets; for example, the paragraph opening tag is written as "<p>". Content follows a start tag that ends with an end tag: tag name starting with a slash; for example, a paragraph end tag is written as "</p>". The first label can be labeled "Opening tag" and the second label can be called the "Closing tag".

Here is the list of some paired tags in HTML:

Open Tag	Close Tag
<div>	</div>
<table>	</table>
<form>	</form>
<span>	</span>
<p>	</p>
<ul>	</ul>
<html>	</html>
<head>	</head>

Unpaired Tags

An HTML tag is called an odd tag if the tag has only an opening tag and no closing tag or accompanying tag. The unpaired tag does not require a closing tag; with this type, an opening label is sufficient. Unpaired tags are also sometimes named single tags or singular tags because they do not require an accompanying tag.

It is to close the unpaired/singular tags. But unfortunately, we do not have the closing tag. So an unpaired tag is closed putting behind a slash (/) before the greater than > sign. For example: <bru />. Below is the list of some unpaired tags in HTML. The use of a slash (/) in the tags is to close them. Here are some examples of unpaired tags.

- Open Tag

  - <hr>

    Example:

    ```
    <!DOCTYPE html>
    <html lang="en">
    <head>
        <title>Document</title>
    </head>
    <body>
        <h1> HTML Unpaired Tags</h1>
        <p> First Para </p>
        <hr>
        <p> Second Para </p>
        </body>
    </html>
    ```

The output of the code is given below.

HTML Unpaired Tags

First Para

Second Para

HTML Unpaired tags.

  - <meta>

Example:

```
<meta charset="UTF-8">
    <meta HTTP-equiv="X-UA-Compatible"
content="IE=edge">
<meta name="viewport" content="width=device-
width, initial-scale=1.0">
```

-

Example:

```
<!DOCTYPE html>
<html lang="en">
<head>
    <title>Document</title>
</head>
<body>
    <h1> HTML Unpaired Tags</h1>
    <p> First Para </p>
    <br>
    <p> Second Para </p>
    </body>
</html>
```

- The output of the code is given below.

HTML Unpaired Tags

First Para

Second Para

HTML Unpaired tags.

- <input>

Example:

```
<!DOCTYPE html>
<html lang="en">
<head>
```

```
    <title>Document</title>
</head>
<body>
    <h1> HTML Unpaired Tags</h1>
    <input type="text" placeholder="Enter the
text">
    <input type="file" >
    <input type="color">
    </body>
</html>
```

The output of the code is given below.

HTML Unpaired Tags

| Enter the text | Choose File No file chosen | ▬ |

HTML Unpaired tags.

Heading Tags (H1 Tag to H6 Tag)

These tags are used to give headings of different sizes in a document. There are six different heading tags, which give various heading sizes and are defined by <h1> – <h6> tags. <h1> gives the biggest heading and <h6> gives the smallest one. So <h1> can be used for important headings for bold headings and <h6> can be used for the least important one.

```
<!DOCTYPE html>
<html lang="en">
<head>
 <meta charset="UTF-8">
 <title> HTML Heading Tag </title>
</head>
<body>
<h1> This is Heading 1 </h1>
 <h2> This is Heading 2 </h2>
<h3> This is Heading 3 </h3>
<h4> This is Heading 4 </h4>
<h5> This is Heading 5 </h5>
<h6> This is Heading 6 </h6>
</body>
</html>
```

HTML p Tag – Paragraph Tag

The <p> tag defines a paragraph in a document. An HTML paragraph or HTML <p> tag provides the text inside the paragraph as completion. It is noteworthy that the browser itself adds line breaks before and after the paragraph.

We'll show you how it works with a simple example.

```
<!DOCTYPE html>
<html lang="en">
<head>
 <meta charset="UTF-8">
 <title> HTML Paragraph Tag </title>
</head>
<body>
<p> This is First Paragraph </p>
 <p> This is Second Paragraph </p>
<p> This is Third Paragraph </p>
</body>
</html>
```

HTML Tag – Anchor Tag

An HTML hyperlink is defined using the <a> tag (Anchor tag). It is used to create a link to any file, web page, image, etc.

This tag is called an anchor tag, and anything between the opening <a> tag and closing </a> tag is a part of the link, and the user can click on that part to go to the linked document.

```
<!DOCTYPE html>
<HTML lang="en">
<head>
 <meta charset="UTF-8">
 <title> Anchor Tag </title>
</head>
<body>
<a target="_blank" href="https://www.google.com"> This is
a link </a>
</body>
</html>
```

HTML img Tag – Image Tag

The img tag is used to add images to HTML documents.[17] The 'src' is used to specify the source of the image. The height and width of the image can control the – height="px" and width="px".

The alt is used as an alternative if the image is not displayed. Whatever is written as the value of this attribute is displayed. It provides information about the image.

```
<!DOCTYPE html>
<html lang="en">
<head>
  <meta charset="UTF-8">
  <title> Image Tag </title>
</head>
<body>
<img src=image-1.png" width="400px" height="200px">
</body>
</html>
```

Self-Closing Tags

Self-closing tags are HTML tags that do not have a partner tag, where the first tag is the only tag needed that is valid for formatting. The main and important information is contained INSIDE the element as its attribute. A "img"tag is a simple example of a self-closing tag. Let's see it in action below.

```
<!DOCTYPE html>
<html lang="en">
<head>
  <meta charset="UTF-8">
  <title> HTML Image Tag </title>
</head>
<body>
<img src="image-1.png" width="400px" height="200px">
</body>
</html>
```

Utility-Based Tags

The HTML tags can be widely differentiated on the basis of utility and on the basis of the purpose they serve. We can divide them into three categories as given below:

- Formatting Tags
- Structure Tags
- Control Tags

The HTML tags that help us in the formatting of the texts like the size of the text, font styles, making a text bold, etc. This is done only using tags like <font>, <b>, <u>, etc. Tables, divisions, and span tags are those tags that help format a web page or document that set the layout of the page. Below is a simple program using divisions for formatting the page along with some other text formatting tags.

```
<html>
<head>
<title> Title </title>
</head>
<body>
<div class="container">
<div class="row">
<div class="col-25">
<label for="email"> <b>Name</b> </label>
</div>
<div class="col-35">
<input type="text" placeholder="First Name"
name="fname" required>
</div>
<div class="col-35">
<input type="text" placeholder="Last Name"
name="lname" required>
</div>
</div>
</div>
</body>
</html>
```

Structure Tags

HTML tags that help structure an HTML document are called Structure Tags.[18] Description, title, HTML, heading, body, etc. form a group of page structure tags. Structure tags only help in building or creating a basic HTML page from the root; that is, they do not affect or participate in text formatting. The basic HTML program is therefore a basic group of structural tags.

Some of the most common HTML5 structural elements are described below.

The <header> tag

This element is used as a container for the page header content. A tag typically contains heading tags (<h1> – <h6>), a logo image, or other content that represents the content. It is possible to have more than one <header> tag per page. However, a <header> cannot be coded within a <footer> tag or another <header> tag.

Example:

```
<!DOCTYPE html>
<html lang="en">
<head>
    <title> HTML </title>
    <style>
        body{
            text-align: center;
            margin:0;
            padding:10px;
            font-size: 20px;
        }
          header{
border:1px solid darkblue;
height:100px;
margin: 2px;
background-color: chocolate;
}
nav{
    border:1px solid darkblue;
height:120px;
margin: 2px;

}
main{
height:200px;
display:flex;
flex-direction: row;
}
.section1{
height:200px;
width:80%;
display:flex;
flex-direction: column;

}
section{
```

```
    border:1px solid darkblue;
    height:120px;
    flex-direction: row;
margin: 2px;
}

article{
    border:1px solid darkblue;
    height:140px;
    flex-direction: row;
    margin: 2px;
}
aside{
    border:1px solid darkblue;
    width:30%;
    margin: 2px;

}
footer{
    border:1px solid darkblue;
height:100px;
margin: 2px;

}

    </style>
  </head>
<body>
    <header>
        Header Tag Content
    </header>
    <nav>
        Navbar Tag Content
    </nav>
    <main>
        <div class="section1">
            <section>
                Section Tag Content

            </section>
            <article>
                Article  Tag Content
```

```
            </article>
        </div>


    <aside>
        Aside Tag Content
    </aside>
    </main>


    <footer>
        Footer Tag Content
    </footer>
    </body>
</html>
```

The output of the code is given below.

| Header Tag Content |
| Navbar Tag Content |
Section Tag Content	Aside Tag Content
Article Tag Content	
Footer Tag Content	

Header tag (with background color).

The <nav> tag
This tag is a block-level element used to define the main blocks of navigation links or navigation menus.

```
<!DOCTYPE html>
<html lang="en">
<head>
    <title> HTML </title>
    <style>
        body{
```

```
            text-align: center;
            margin:0;
            padding:10px;
            font-size: 20px;
        }
          header{
border:1px solid darkblue;
height:100px;
margin: 2px;
}
nav{
    border:1px solid darkblue;
height:120px;
margin: 2px;
background-color: chocolate;

}
main{
height:200px;
display:flex;
flex-direction: row;
}
.section1{
height:200px;
width:80%;
display:flex;
flex-direction: column;

}
section{
    border: 1px solid darkblue;
    height: 120px;
    flex-direction: row;
margin: 2px;
}

article{
    border:1px solid darkblue;
    height: 140px;
    flex-direction: row;
    margin: 2px;
}
```

```
aside{
    border:1px solid darkblue;
    width:30%;
    margin: 2px;

}
footer{
    border: 1px solid darkblue;
height: 100px;
margin: 2px;

}

    </style>
 </head>
<body>
    <header>
        Header Tag Content
    </header>
    <nav>
        Navbar Tag Content
    </nav>
    <main>
        <div class="section1">
            <section>
                Section Tag Content

            </section>
            <article>
                Article Tag Content
            </article>
        </div>


    <aside>
        Aside Tag Content
    </aside>
    </main>
    <footer>
        Footer Tag Content
    </footer>
    </body>
</html>
```

The output of the code is given below.

Navbar tag (with background color).

The <main> tag

It is used to display a container for the main page content that is not repeated in other parts of the page. A web page can contain only one <main> element. Additionally, it cannot be included as a child element in a <header>, <nav>, footer>, <article>, or <aside> tag.

Example:

```
<!DOCTYPE html>
<html lang="en">
<head>
    <title> HTML </title>
    <style>
        body{
            text-align: center;
            margin: 0;
            padding:10px;
            font-size: 20px;
        }
            header{
border: 1px solid darkblue;
height: 100px;
margin: 2px;
}
nav{
    border: 1px solid darkblue;
height: 120px;
margin: 2px;

}
```

```
main{
height: 200px;
display: flex;
flex-direction: row;
background-color: chocolate;

}
.section1{
height:200px;
width:80%;
display: flex;
flex-direction: column;

}
section{
    border: 1px solid darkblue;
    height: 120px;
    flex-direction: row;
margin: 2px;
}

article{
    border: 1px solid darkblue;
    height: 140px;
    flex-direction: row;
    margin: 2px;
}
aside{
    border: 1px solid darkblue;
    width:30%;
    margin: 2px;

}
footer{
    border: 1px solid darkblue;
height:100px;
margin: 2px;

}

    </style>
  </head>
<body>
    <header>
```

```
            Header Tag Content
    </header>
    <nav>
        Navbar Tag Content
    </nav>
    <main>
        <div class="section1">
            <section>
                Section Tag Content

            </section>
            <article>
                Article Tag Content
            </article>
        </div>


    <aside>
        Aside Tag Content
    </aside>
    </main>
    <footer>
        Footer Tag Content
    </footer>
    </body>
</html>
```

The output of the code is given below.

Main tag (with background color).

<section> tag

The <section> tag defines general sections of a web page, such as headers, footers, or any other parts of a document. In this context, a section is a thematic grouping of content.

Example:

```
<!DOCTYPE html>
<html lang="en">
<head>
    <title> HTML </title>
    <style>
        body{
            text-align: center;
            margin: 0;
            padding:10px;
            font-size: 20px;
        }
        header{
border: 1px solid darkblue;
height: 100px;
margin: 2px;
}
nav{
    border: 1px solid darkblue;
height: 120px;
margin: 2px;

}
main{
height: 200px;
display: flex;
flex-direction: row;

}
.section1{
height: 200px;
width:80%;
display: flex;
flex-direction: column;

}
```

```
section{
    border: 1px solid darkblue;
    height: 120px;
    flex-direction: row;
margin: 2px;
background-color: chocolate;

}

article{
    border: 1px solid darkblue;
    height :140px;
    flex-direction: row;
    margin: 2px;  .
}
aside{
    border: 1px solid darkblue;
    width:30%;
    margin: 2px;

}
footer{
    border: 1px solid darkblue;
height:100px;
margin: 2px;

}

    </style>
  </head>
<body>
    <header>
        Header Tag Content
    </header>
    <nav>
        Navbar Tag Content
    </nav>
    <main>
        <div class="section1">
            <section>
                Section Tag Content

            </section>
```

```
            <article>
                 Article   Tag Content
            </article>
        </div>


    <aside>
        Aside Tag Content
    </aside>
    </main>
    <footer>
        Footer Tag Content
    </footer>
    </body>
</html>
```

The output of the code is given below.

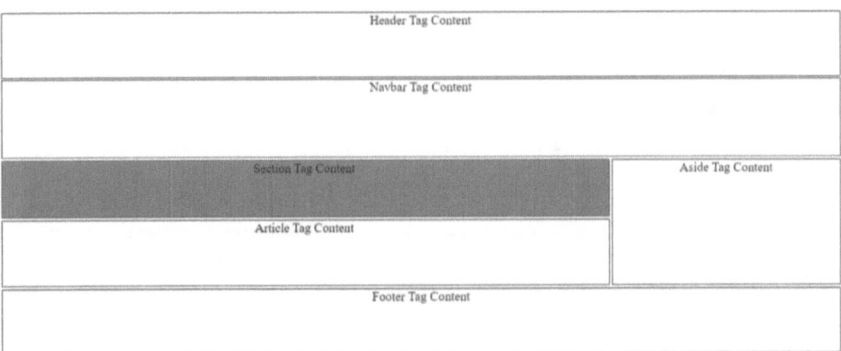

Section tag (with background color).

<article> tag

The <article> element represents a complete or self-contained composition in a document, page, application, or website that is essentially self-distributable or reusable.

Example:

```
<!DOCTYPE html>
<html lang="en">
<head>
    <title> HTML </title>
```

```
<style>
    body{
        text-align: center;
        margin:0;
        padding:10px;
        font-size: 20px;
    }
     header{
border: 1px solid darkblue;
height:100px;
margin: 2px;
}
nav{
    border:1px solid darkblue;
height:120px;
margin: 2px;

}
main{
height:200px;
display: flex;
flex-direction: row;

}
.section1{
height: 200px;
width: 80%;
display: flex;
flex-direction: column;

}
section{
    border:1px solid darkblue;
    height:120px;
    flex-direction: row;
margin: 2px;

}

article{
    border: 1px solid darkblue;
    height: 140px;
    flex-direction: row;
```

```
    margin: 2px;
    background-color: chocolate;

}
aside{
    border: 1px solid darkblue;
    width:30%;
    margin: 2px;

}
footer{
    border: 1px solid darkblue;
height:100px;
margin: 2px;

}

    </style>
  </head>
<body>
    <header>
        Header Tag Content
    </header>
    <nav>
        Navbar Tag Content
    </nav>
    <main>
        <div class="section1">
            <section>
                Section Tag Content

            </section>
            <article>
                Article Tag Content
            </article>
        </div>


    <aside>
        Aside Tag Content
    </aside>
    </main>
```

```
    <footer>
        Footer Tag Content
    </footer>
    </body>
</html>
```

The output of the code is given below.

Article tag (with background color).

<aside> tag

The <aside> tag is a block-level element that defines content apart from the content it is placed within. The content on the page should be related to the surrounding content.

Example:

```
<!DOCTYPE html>
<html lang="en">
<head>
    <title> HTML </title>
    <style>
        body{
            text-align: center;
            margin:0;
            padding:10px;
            font-size: 20px;
        }
            header{
border: 1px solid darkblue;
height: 100px;
margin: 2px;
}
```

```
nav{
    border: 1px solid darkblue;
height: 120px;
margin: 2px;

}
main{
height: 200px;
display: flex;
flex-direction: row;

}
.section1{
height: 200px;
width: 80%;
display: flex;
flex-direction: column;

}
section{
    border: 1px solid darkblue;
    height: 120px;
    flex-direction: row;
margin: 2px;

}

article{
    border: 1px solid darkblue;
    height: 140px;
    flex-direction: row;
    margin: 2px;

}
aside{
    border:1px solid darkblue;
    width:30%;
    margin: 2px;
    background-color: chocolate;
}
footer{
    border: 1px solid darkblue;
height: 100px;
```

```
margin: 2px;

}

    </style>
  </head>
<body>
    <header>
        Header Tag Content
    </header>
    <nav>
        Navbar Tag Content
    </nav>
    <main>
        <div class="section1">
            <section>
                Section Tag Content

            </section>
            <article>
                Article Tag Content
            </article>
        </div>
  <aside>
        Aside Tag Content
    </aside>
    </main>
    <footer>
        Footer Tag Content
    </footer>
    </body>
</html>
```

The output of the code is given below.

| Header Tag Content |
| Navbar Tag Content |
| Section Tag Content / Article Tag Content | Aside Tag Content |
| Footer Tag Content |

Aside tag (with background color).

<footer> tag

The <footer> tag is a block-level element that defines footer information for an entire web page or document section. The <footer> content usually consists of contact information, copyright, links, or logos. In some cases, a web page may contain multiple <footer> tags.

Example:

```
<!DOCTYPE html>
<html lang="en">
<head>
    <title> HTML </title>
    <style>
        body{
            text-align: center;
            margin:0;
            padding:10px;
            font-size: 20px;
        }
            header{
border:1px solid darkblue;
height:100px;
margin: 2px;
}
nav{
    border:1px solid darkblue;
height:120px;
margin: 2px;

}
main{
height:200px;
display:flex;
flex-direction: row;

}
.section1{
height: 200px;
width:80%;
display: flex;
flex-direction: column;

}
```

```css
section{
    border: 1px solid darkblue;
    height: 120px;
    flex-direction: row;
margin: 2px;

}

article{
    border: 1px solid darkblue;
    height: 140px;
    flex-direction: row;
    margin: 2px;

}
aside{
    border: 1px solid darkblue;
    width: 30%;
    margin: 2px;
}
footer{
    border: 1px solid darkblue;
height:100px;
margin: 2px;
background-color: chocolate;

}

    </style>
 </head>
<body>
    <header>
        Header Tag Content
    </header>
    <nav>
        Navbar Tag Content
    </nav>
    <main>
        <div class="section1">
            <section>
                Section Tag Content

            </section>
```

```
        <article>
            Article   Tag Content
        </article>
    </div>
<aside>
    Aside Tag Content
  </aside>
  </main>
  <footer>
      Footer Tag Content
  </footer>
  </body>
</html>
```

The output of the code is given below.

Footer side tag (with background color).

<figure> tag

The <figure> tag specifies standalone content, such as illustrations, diagrams, photos, or pieces of code. By default, this is a block-level element with a right and left margin setting of 40 pixels.

Example:

```
<!DOCTYPE html>
<html lang="en">
<head>
    <title> HTML </title>
    <style>
        body{
```

```
            text-align: center;
            margin: 0;
            padding: 10px;
            font-size: 20px;
        }
          header{
border: 1px solid darkblue;
height: 100px;
margin: 2px;
}
nav{
    border: 1px solid darkblue;
height: 120px;
margin: 2px;

}
main{
height: 200px;
display: flex;
flex-direction: row;

}
.section1{
height: 200px;
width: 80%;
display: flex;
flex-direction: column;

}
section{
    border: 1px solid darkblue;
    height: 120px;
    flex-direction: row;
margin: 2px;

}

article{
    border: 1px solid darkblue;
    height: 140px;
    flex-direction: row;
    margin: 2px;

}
```

```
aside{
    border: 1px solid darkblue;
    width: 30%;
    margin: 2px;
}
footer{
    border: 1px solid darkblue;
height: 100px;
margin: 2px;
background-color: chocolate;

}

    </style>
 </head>
<body>
    <figure>
        <h2> Figure Tag with Figcaption </h2>
        <img src="https://images.pexels.com/
photos/56866/garden-rose-red-pink-56866.jpeg?auto=
compress&cs=tinysrgbw=600" alt="flamingo">
        <figcaption><i>fig. 1</i> A pink Flower.
</figcaption>
        </figure>
</body>
</html>
```

The output of the code is given below.

Figure Tag with Figcaption

fig. 1 A pink Flower.

<figure> tag.

<figcaption> tag

<figcaption> is a block-level tag that defines a caption for the <figure> element discussed in the previous section. The <figcaption> tag is normally encoded as the first or last child element of the <figure> tag.

Example:

```
<!DOCTYPE html>
<html lang="en">
<head>
    <title> HTML </title>
    <style>
        body{
            text-align: center;
            margin:0;
            padding:10px;
            font-size: 20px;
        }
          header{
border: 1px solid darkblue;
height: 100px;
margin: 2px;
}
nav{
    border: 1px solid darkblue;
height: 120px;
margin: 2px;

}
main{
height: 200px;
display: flex;
flex-direction: row;

}
.section1{
height: 200px;
width:80%;
display: flex;
flex-direction: column;

}
```

```
section{
    border: 1px solid darkblue;
    height: 120px;
    flex-direction: row;
margin: 2px;

}

article{
    border: 1px solid darkblue;
    height: 140px;
    flex-direction: row;
    margin: 2px;

}
aside{
    border: 1px solid darkblue;
    width: 30%;
    margin: 2px;
}
footer{
    border: 1px solid darkblue;
height: 100px;
margin: 2px;
background-color: chocolate;

}

    </style>
  </head>
<body>
    <figure>
        <h2> Figure Tag with Figcaption </h2>
        <img src="https://images.pexels.com/
photos/56866/garden-rose-red-pink-56866.jpeg?auto=
compress&cs=tinysrgb&w=600" alt="flamingo">
        <figcaption><i>fig. 1</i> A pink Flower.
</figcaption>
        </figure>
</body>
</html>
```

Control Tags

Another category of tags that can be created is 'Control Tags'. Script tags, radio buttons or checkboxes, Form tags, etc. are control tags. These are tags that are used when managing content or managing scripts or libraries that are external. All form tags, dropdowns, input text fields, etc. are used when interacting with a visitor or user.

The HTML tags are based on the type of tags and their usefulness. HTML tags can also be easily divided based on basic categories such as basic root tags, text formatting tags, audio and video tags, form and input tags, frames, links, lists, tables, styles, meta tags, etc.

HTML Tag List

There are various tags in HTML. You will get tags in alphabetical order below.[19]

Tags	Description
<!--...-->	It describes a comment text in the source code
<!doctype>	It defines a document type
<a>	It specifies an anchor (Hyperlink)
	It is used for link in internal/external web documents
<abbr>	It describes an abbreviation (acronyms)
<acronym>	It describes an acronyms
<address>	It describes an address information
<applet>	It describes embedding an applet in HTML document
<area>	It defines an area in an image map
<article>	It defines an article
<aside>	It describes contain set
<audio>	It specifies audio content
<b>	It specifies text weight in bold
<base>	It defines a URL base for all the links within a web page
<basefont>	It describes a default font color, size, and face in a document
<bb>	It defines browser command that invokes as per client action
<bdo>	It specifies direction of text display
<big>	It defines a big text
<blockquote>	It specifies a long quotation
<body>	It specifies a main section (body) part in HTML document
 	It specifies a single-line break
<button>	It specifies a press/push button
<canvas>	It specifies the display of graphics on HTML web document
<caption>	It specifies a table caption
<center>	It specifies a text is display in center align
<cite>	It specifies a text citation
<code>	It specifies computer code text
<col>	It specifies a column within a <colgroup> element in table
<colgroup>	It specifies a group of more than one column inside table
<command>	It specifies a command button that invokes as per user action

(Continued)

Tags	Description
<datagrid>	It specifies a represent data in Datagrid either list wise or tree wise
<datalist>	It specifies a list of predefined options for an <input> element that used to provide an "autocomplete" feature for <input> elements. The <datalist> id attribute should be equal to the <input> element's list attribute
<dd>	It specifies a definition description in a definition list
<del>	It specifies text deleted in web document
<details>	It specifies an additional details hide or show as per user action
<dfn>	It specifies a definition team
<dialog>	It specifies a chat conversation between one or more persons
<dir>	It specifies a directory list
<div>	It specifies a division part
<dl>	It specifies a definition list
<dt>	It specifies a definition team
<em>	It specifies a text is in emphasized format
<embed>	It defines a embedding external application using a relative plug-in
<eventsource>	It defines a source of event generated to remote server
<fieldset>	It defines a grouping of related form elements
<figcaption>	It defines a caption text corresponding with a figure element
<figure>	It defines self-contained content corresponding with a <figcaption> element
<font>	It defines a font size, font face, and font color for its text
<footer>	It defines a footer section containing details about the author, copyright, contact us, sitemap, or links to related documents
<frame>	It defines frame window
<frameset>	It is used to hold one or more <frame> elements
<form>	It defines a form section that has interactive input controls to submit form information to a server
<h1> to <h6>	It defines heading levels from 1 to 6 of different sizes
<head>	It defines header section of HTML document. It defines as a container that holds introductory content or navigation links
<header>	It describes the heading of a section that holds the h1 to h6 tags
<hgroup>	<hr /> It represents a thematic break between paragraph-level tags. It typically draws a horizontal line
<html>	It defines a document as an HTML markup language
<i>	It defines an italic format text
<iframe>	It defines an inline frame that embedded external content into the current web document
<img>	It is used to insert image into a web document
<input>	It defines to get information in selected input
<ins>	It is used to indicate text that is inserted into a page and indicates changes to a document
<isindex>	It is used to create a single-line search prompt for querying the contents of the document
<kbd>	It is used to identify text that represents keyboard input
<keygen>	It is used to generate a signed certificate, which is used to authenticate services

(Continued)

Tags	Description
<label>	It is used to caption a text label with a form <input> element
<legend>	It is used to add a caption (title) to a group of related form elements that are grouped together into the <fieldset> tag
<li>	It defines a list item either as an ordered list or unordered list
<link>	It is used to load external stylesheets into HTML document
<map>	It defines a clickable image map
<mark>	It is used to highlight (marked) specific text
<menu>	It is used to display an unordered list of items/menu of commands
<meta>	It is used to provide structured metadata about a web page
<meter>	It is used to measure data within a given range
<nav>	It is used to define a group of navigation links
<noframes>	It used to provide a fallback content to the browser that does not support the <frame> element
<noscript>	It is used to provide a fall-back content to the browser that does not support the JavaScript
<object>	It is used to embed objects such as images, audio, videos, Java applets, and Flash animations
<ol>	It defines an ordered list of items
<optgroup>	It is used to create a grouping of options, the related options are grouped under specific headings
<option>	It represents option items within a <select>, <optgroup>, or <datalist> element
<output>	It is used for representing the result of a calculation
<p>	It is used to represent a paragraph text
<param>	It provides parameters for embedded object element
<pre>	It is used to represent preformatted text
<progress>	It represents the progress of a task
<q>	It represents the short quotation
<rp>	It is used to provide parentheses around fall-back content to the browser that does not support the ruby annotations
<rt>	It specifies the ruby text of ruby annotation
<ruby>	It is used to represent a ruby annotation
<s>	The text displays in a strikethrough style
<samp>	It represents text that should be interpreted as sample output from a computer program
<script>	It defines client-side JavaScript
<section>	It divides a document into a number of different generic sections
<select>	It is used to create a drop-down list
<small>	It is used to make the text one size smaller
<source>	It is used to specify multiple media resources
<span>	It is used to group and apply styles to inline elements
<strike>	It represents strikethrough text
<strong>	It represents strong emphasis greater important text
<style>	It is used to add CSS style to an HTML document
<sub>	It represents inline subscript text
<sup>	It defines inline superscript text

(Continued)

Tags	Description
<table>	It is used to define a table in an HTML document
<tbody>	It is used for grouping table rows
<td>	It is used to create standard data cell in an HTML table
<textarea>	It creates a multiline text input
<tfoot>	It is used to add a footer to a table that contains a summary of the table data
<th>	It is used to create header of a group of cell in an HTML table
<thead>	It is used to add a header to a table that contains header information of the table
<time>	It represents the date and/or time in an HTML document
<title>	It represents title of an HTML document
<tr>	It represents a row of cells in a table
<track>	It defines text tracks for both the <audio> and <video> tags
<tt>	It defines teletype text
<u>	It defines underlined text
<ul>	It defines an unordered list of items
<var>	It defines a variable in a computer program or mathematical equation
<video>	It is used to embed video content
<wbr>	It defines a word break opportunity

WHAT IS AN HTML EDITOR?

An editor is software for creating and editing HTML code.[20] It can be standalone software designed for writing and editing code or part of an Integrated Development Environment (IDE). The HTML editor provides more advanced features and is specially designed for developers to create websites more efficiently. It ensures that every line of code is clean and working properly.

There are several professional editors that web developers use for coding. However, not every editor can satisfy all your needs. A good HTML editor must therefore have the following features:

- syntax highlighting – display of text, especially source code, in different colors and fonts,

- tab display support – keep multiple web pages open in tabs at the same time,

- checking for errors in the HTML document,

- code wrapping – hiding large code fragments leaving only a line.

Some HTML editors can also translate HTML into a programming language such as CSS, XML, or JavaScript. This means that different types of HTML editors can offer different sets of functions and features.

The most popular HTML editors are listed below:

- WebStorm

- Visual Studio Code

- Atom

- Sublime text

- Notepad++

- HTML-Kit

- CoffeeCup

- Bluefish

- Sublime

HTML COMMENTS

The comments are usually added with the purpose of making the source code easier to understand. It may help other developers to understand what you were trying to do with the HTML. Comments are not displayed in the browser.

Syntax:

```
<!-- Comments here -->
```

An HTML comment starts with <!-- and ends with --> as shown in the example below:

```
<!-- This is an HTML comment -->
<!-- This is a multiline HTML comment
 !-- This is a multiline HTML commentmple
 omme<p>This is a normal text.</p>
```

The comment tag is useful when debugging code.

- This is a simple piece of code that web browsers delete (ignore), i.e. the browser does not display it.

- It helps the coder and the reader to understand the part of code used especially in complex source code.

TYPES OF HTML COMMENTS

There are three types of comments in HTML:[21]

- Single line comment: A single line comment is given inside a tag (<!– comment ->). Example,

```
<!DOCTYPE html>
<html lang="en">
<head>
    <title> HTML </title>
    <style>
        body{
            text-align: center;
            margin:0;
            padding:10px;
            font-size: 20px;
        }

    </style>
  </head>
<body>
        <h2> HTML Comments </h2>

<!-- The following code is a paragraph-->
<p> Here you are learning multiline HTML Comments
</p>

<!-- The following code is a Heading-->
<p> Here you are learning single HTML Comments </
p>
</body>
</html>
```

Multiline comment: This comment can be given by the syntax (<!– ->), basically it is the same as used in a single line comment, the difference is half of the comment part (" -> "), is appended where to intended the comment line ends. Example,

```
<!DOCTYPE html>
<html lang="en">
<head>
    <title> HTML </title>
    <style>
        body{
            text-align: center;
            margin:0;
            padding:10px;
            font-size: 20px;
        }

    </style>
  </head>
<body>
        <h2> HTML Comments </h2>
<!--Comments can be used to
add multiple line
on to the HTML Document.-->
<p> Here you are learning multiline HTML Comments
</p>
</body>
</html>
```

- Using the <comment> tag: There used to be an HTML <comment> tag, but it is currently not supported by any modern browser. Example,

```
<!DOCTYPE html>
<html lang="en">
<head>
    <title> HTML </title>
    <style>
        body{
            text-align: center;
            margin:0;
            padding:10px;
```

```
            font-size: 20px;
        }

    </style>
  </head>
<body>
        <h2> HTML Comments </h2>

        <p>
            Only HTML <comment>not</comment>
            CSS
        </p>
</body>
</html>
```

Importance:

- It improves code readability, especially when multiple developers access a single HTML document.

- It ensures fast and efficient understanding of complex codes.

- It makes debugging the source code easier and makes it easier to maintain.

HTML TAG VS. ELEMENT

Tag

HTML tags and elements are sometimes recognized as the same thing.[22] But it's not. HTML elements and tags have subtle differences that many people are unaware of.

HTML tags are the common building blocks of HTML pages. It tells the browser how to present content to the user. A tag begins with a < bracket and ends with a > bracket. In HTML, most tags exist in pairs. A tag has a beginning part and an ending part. They are similar, except there is a / character after the opening parenthesis in the closing part.

Syntax:

```
Opening tag: <TagName>
Closing tag: </TagName>
```

Example:

```
<!DOCTYPE html>
<html lang="en">
<head>
    <title> HTML </title>
    <style>
        body{
            margin:0;
            padding:50px;
            font-size: 20px;
        }
        table, tr, td, th{
        border:2px solid black;
        }

    </style>
 </head>
<body>
    <h1> Main Heading </h1>
    <p> <strong>Paragraph</strong> </p>
    <p>Lorem ipsum dolor oo sit amet, consectetur
adipiscing elit. Nam tellus exi, posuere at mauris
sed, ullamcorper aefficitur augue. Phasellus eros
magna, fringilla in maalesuada sed, palacerat id
sem. Duis sodales mi id quaam lobortis semper.
Integer tisncidunt neque arcu, et tincidunt magna
posuere pretiuam. Mauris nec pretium ipsum. Sed
bibendum, sem sed elemeantum tincidunt, arcu ipsum
pellentesque eanim, sed tempor nibh metus
pellentesque libero.</p>

    <table>
        <tr>
            <th> Serial No </th>
            <th> Name </th>
        </tr>
        <tr>
            <td> 1 </td>
            <td> A </td>
        </tr>
        <tr>
```

```
            <td> 2 </td>
            <td> B </td>
        </tr>
        <tr>
            <td>3</td>
            <td> C </td>
        </tr>
    </table>
</body>
</html>
```

All the <tag> and </tag> used above are referred as tags.

Element

HTML elements include start tags, content, and end tags. HTML elements are part of a website. Let's say you created a div block and entered some text into it. A div filled with text then becomes a component of the HTML page. A tag, along with the content within it, becomes a component and an HTML element. This will be rendered and displayed to the user.

Example:

```
<!DOCTYPE html>
<html lang="en">
<head>
    <title> HTML </title>
    <style>
        body{
            margin:0;
            padding:50px;
            font-size: 20px;
        }


    </style>
  </head>
<body>
    <h1> Main Heading </h1>
    <p> <strong>Paragraph</strong> </p>
</body>
</html>
```

Key Points

Tags	Elements
It consists of an opening and closing bracket	It consists of a starting, content, and an end tag
It consists of reserved keywords that have a unique meaning	It consists of a generalized component that user wants to display on their HTML page
They cannot be nested	They can be nested

TYPES OF ELEMENTS

- Block Level: These elements are intended to structure the main part of the page by dividing the content into full-width blocks.[23]

  - paragraphs <p>

  - lists: <ul>, <ol>, and <li>

  - headings <h1> to <h6>

  - articles <article>

  - sections <section>

  - long quotes <blockquote>

  - Division <div>

  - Form <form>

  - Table <table>

- Inline Level: These elements are meant to differentiate part of some text, to give it a particular meaning. Inline elements usually comprise a single or few words.

  - links <a>

  - image <img>

  - span <span>

  - button <button>

  - input <input>

  - label <label>

- textarea <textarea>

- emphasised words <em>

- important words <strong>

- short quotes <q>

- Strong <strong>

TYPES OF HTML ELEMENTS

Elements can be placed in two different groups such as block-level elements and row-level elements.[24] The former forms the structure of the document, while the latter dresses the contents of the block.

The block element also takes up 100% of the available width and is rendered with line breaks before and after. Whereas an inline element only takes up as much space as it needs.

The most commonly used block-level elements are <div>, <p>, <h1> to <h6>, <form>, <ol>, <ul>, <li>, etc. The commonly used row-level elements are <img>, <a>, <span>, <strong>, <b>, <em>, <i>, <code>, <input>, <button>, etc.

HTML ELEMENT SYNTAX

An HTML element is a separate part of an HTML document. It represents semantics or meaning. For example, the title element represents the title of the document.

Most HTML elements start with a start tag (or opening tag) and an end tag (or closing tag), with content in between. Elements can also contain attributes that define their other properties.

HTML uses tags for its syntax. The tag consists of special characters: <, >, and /. They are interpreted by software to create an HTML element.

```
<p class="text"> This is a paragraph </p>
```

EMPTY HTML ELEMENTS

Empty elements (also called self-closing, void elements) are not container tags, you cannot write <hr>here is your some content</hr> or
some content</br>.[25] A common example is the <br> element, which represents a line break. Some other common empty elements are <img>, <meta>, <input>, <link>, <hr>, etc.

Example:

```
<p>This paragraph contains break tag <br> that
break line. </p>
<img src="images-1.jpg" alt=" Keyword of image ">
<input type="text" name="user_name">
```

NESTING HTML ELEMENTS

Most HTML elements can contain a number of further elements, which are made up of tags, attributes, and content or other elements.

Example:

```
<!DOCTYPE HTML>
<html>
  <head>
    <meta content="text/HTML;  HTTP-
equiv="Content-Type"  charset=utf-8">
    <title>Title of the document</title>
    <style>
    Body {
      width:500px;
      margin:0 auto,
    }
    </style>
  </head>

  <body>
    <h1> Nesting HTML Elements </h1>
    p> This is a paragraph that contain <b>bold</b>
text.</p>
    <p>This is a paragraph that contain  <em>
emphasized </em> text. </p>
    <p>This is a paragraph that contain  <mark>
highlighted </mark> text. </p>

</html>
```

CASE INSENSITIVITY IN TAGS

There are some tag and attribute names that are not case-sensitive (but most attribute values are case-sensitive). It means the tags <P> and <p> define the same thing in HTML, which is a paragraph. But in XHTML, they are case-sensitive and the tag <P> is different from the tag <p>.

Example:

```
<!DOCTYPE HTML>
<html>
  <head>
    <meta HTTP-equiv="Content-Type" content="text/
HTML; charset=utf-8">
    <title>Title of the document</title>
    <style>
    body{
      width:500px;
      margin:0 auto,
    }
    </style>
  </head>

  <body>
    <h1> Case Insensitivity in Tags and Attributes
</h1>
    <p> This is a paragraph. </p>
<P> This is also paragraph. </P>
  </body>
</html>
```

HTML ATTRIBUTES

An element's attributes are expressed within the element's start tag.[26] Attributes have a name and its value. There should be no more than one attribute with the same case-insensitive name in the same start tag. HTML elements have attributes.

The attributes can be specified in four different ways:

- empty attribute syntax

- unquoted value syntax

- single-quoted value syntax

- double-quoted value syntax

Empty Attribute Syntax

Certain attributes could be specified by providing just the attribute name, with no value.

For example, the disabled attribute is given with the empty attribute syntax such as,

```
<input disabled>
```

Unquoted Value Syntax

Actually there are many tags with attributes with no values such as <input type="text" name="country" value="Norway" readonly> this is valid HTML syntax as attributes have no values.

```
<input type=text value=   readonly>
```

These are additional values that configure the element or adjust the element's behavior in various ways to meet the user's desired criteria.[27]

GENERAL ATTRIBUTES

There are some attributes, such as id, style, title, class, etc., that you can use on the majority of HTML elements.[28] The following section describes their usages.

The id Attribute

It is used to give a unique name or identifier to an element within a document. It makes it easier to select the element using CSS or JavaScript.

```
<!DOCTYPE html>
<html lang="en">
<head>
    <meta charset="UTF-8">
    <meta HTTP-equiv="X-UA-Compatible"
content="IE=edge">
    <meta content="width=device-width, initial-
scale=1.0" name="viewport" >
    <title>Document</title>
</head>
<body>
    <input type="text" id="firstName">
    <div id="container">Some content</div>
    <p id="info text">This is a paragraph.</p>
</body>
</html>
```

The class Attribute

Same as id attribute, the class attribute is also used to identify elements. But unlike id, the class attribute doesn't have to be unique in the HTML document. It means you can apply the same class to multiple elements in a document, as shown in the following example,

```
<!DOCTYPE html>
<html lang="en">
<head>
    <meta charset="UTF-8">
    <meta HTTP-equiv="X-UA-Compatible"
content="IE=edge">
    <meta name="viewport" content="width=device-width,
initial-scale=1.0">
    <title>Document</title>
</head>
<body>
    <input type="text" class="highlight">
    <div class="box highlight">Some content</div>
    <p class="highlight">This is a paragraph.</p>
</body>
</html>
```

The title Attribute

It is used to provide text about an element or its content. The following example is to understand how it actually works.

```
<!DOCTYPE html>
<html lang="en">
<head>
    <meta charset="UTF-8">
    <meta HTTP-equiv="X-UA-Compatible"
content="IE=edge">
    <meta name="viewport" content="width=device-width,
initial-scale=1.0">
    <title>Document</title>
</head>
<body>
    <abbr title="WorldWideWeb Consortium"> W3C </abbr>
    <a href="images-kites.jpg" title="Click to view a
larger image">
```

```
            <img src="images/kites-thumb.jpg" alt="kites">
    </a>
</body>
</html>
```

The style Attribute

It allows to specify CSS styling rules such as color, font, border, etc. within the element. Let's check an example to see how it works.

```
<!DOCTYPE html>
<html lang="en">
<head>
    <meta charset="UTF-8">
    <meta HTTP-equiv="X-UA-Compatible"
content="IE=edge">
    <meta name="viewport" content="width=device-width,
initial-scale=1.0">
    <title>Document</title>
</head>
<body>
    <p style="color: blue;">This is a paragraph.</p>
    <img src="images/sky.jpg" style="width: 200px;"
alt="Cloudy Sky">
    <div style="border: 1px solid red;">Some content
</div>
</body>
</html>
```

ANATOMY OF AN HTML ELEMENT

Let's explore these elements a little further. The main parts of the element are as follows:[29]

- **Opening tag:** It consists of the name of the element (in this case p), wrapped in opening and closing curly braces. It is where the element begins or takes effect – in this case, the paragraph begins.

- **Closing tag:** It is similar to the opening tag, that it includes a slash before the element name. It is used where the element ends – in this case, where the paragraph ends.

- **Content:** It is the data of the element, that is just text.

- **Element:** The opening tag, closing tag, and content together form an element.

Example:

```html
<!DOCTYPE HTML>
<html>
  <head>
    <meta content="text/HTML; HTTP-equiv="Content-
Type" charset=utf-8">
    <title>Title of the document</title>
    <style>
    body{
      width:500px;
      margin:0 auto;
      background-color: YellowGreen;
    }
    h1 { color: blue; }
img{
    width: 200px;
    height: 200px;
}

    </style>
  </head>

  <body>
   <h1> HTML Sample </h1>
   <!DOCTYPE html>
<html lang="en-US">
  <head>
    <meta charset="utf-8">
    <meta name="viewport"
content="width=device-width">
    <title>My test page</title>
  </head>
  <body>
    <p> This is a simple paragraph </p>
    <img src="https://images.pexels.com/
photos/11858609/pexels-photo-11858609.jpeg?auto=co
```

```
mpress&cs=tinysrgb&w=300&lazy=load" alt="My test
image">
  </body>
</html>
```

Here we have the following:

- <!DOCTYPE html> – document type. It is a mandatory preamble. Back in the mists of time when HTML was still young (around 1991/1992), doctypes were supposed to act as references to a set of rules that an HTML page follows to consider good HTML, which mean automatic error checking and other things. However, these days they do not do more and basically just needed to make your document behave properly. That's all need to know for now.

- <html> </html> – <html> element. This element wraps all content on the entire page and is sometimes called the root element. It also contains the lang attribute that sets the primary language of the document.

- <head> </head> – <head> element. This element acts as a container for any content you want to include in your HTML page that isn't the content you're displaying to your page viewers. This includes things like keywords and page description to appear in search results, CSS to style our content, character set declarations, and more.

- <meta charset="utf-8"> – This element sets the character set your document should use to UTF-8, which includes characters from the vast majority of written languages. Basically, it can now handle any textual content you place on it. It has no reason not to set this up and it may help you avoid some problems later on.

- <meta name="viewport" content="width= 'device-width'> – This viewport element ensures that the page is rendered to the width of the viewport, preventing mobile browsers from rendering pages wider than the viewport and then scaling them down.

- <title> </title> – <title> element. It sets the title of the page, which is the name that will appear in the browser tab in which the page is loaded. It is used to describe the page when bookmark/favorite it.

- <body> </body> – <body> element. It contains all the content you want to display to web users when they visit your page, whether it's text, images, videos, games, playable audio tracks, or anything else.

Elements can have attributes that look like the ones below.

```
<p class="note"> This is an important note </p>
```

Attributes contain additional information about an element that you don't want to appear in the actual content. Class here is the name of the attribute and editor note is the value of the attribute. The class attribute allows you to give an element a nonunique identifier that can be used to target it with style information and more.

The attribute should always have the following:

- The space between it and the element name (or the preceding attribute if the element already has one or more attributes).

- Attribute name followed by an equal sign.

- Attribute value wrapped in opening and closing quotes.

SEMANTICS OF EMBEDDED TEXT

Use HTML inline text semantics to define the meaning, structure, or style of a word, line, or any text.

<a> The <a> element (or anchor element) with href attribute creates a hyperlink to pages, files, emails, locations on the particular page, or anything else that a URL can address.

Example:

```
<!DOCTYPE html>
<html>
<head>
<style>
nav {
  list-style-type: none;
  margin: 0;
  padding: 0px;
  overflow: hidden;
  background-color: lightgray;
}

li {
  float: left;
    border-right: 1px solid blue;
}
```

```
li a {
  display: block;
  color: blue;
 font-size:20px;
  text-align: center;
  padding: 10px 20px;
  text-decoration: none;
}
.active{
background-color: gray;
color: white;
}
li a:hover {
  background-color: orange;
  color: white;
}

</style>
</head>
<body>


<header>
    <h2> Nav Tag </h2>
    <nav>
        <li><a class="active" href="#home">Home
</a></li>
        <li><a href="#">Java</a></li>
        <li><a href="#">HTML</a></li>
        <li><a href="#">CSS</a></li>
      </nav>
   </header>

</body>
</html>
```

Nav Tag

Home	Java	HTML	CSS	

Tag <a>.

<abbr> The <abbr> element defines an abbreviation or acronym.

Example:

```
<!DOCTYPE html>
<html>
<head>
<style>
nav {
  list-style-type: none;
  margin: 0;
  padding: 0px;
  overflow: hidden;
  background-color: lightgray;
}

li {
  float: left;
    border-right: 1px solid blue;
}

li a {
  display: block;
  color: blue;
 font-size:20px;
  text-align: center;
  padding: 10px 20px;
  text-decoration: none;
}
.active{
background-color: gray;
color: white;
}
li a:hover {
  background-color: orange;
  color: white;
}

</style>
</head>
<body>
<h2> Paragraph tag </h2>
  <p>You can use <abbr>CSS</abbr> (Cascading Style
Sheets) to style your <abbr>HTML</abbr> (HyperText
Markup Language). <br>  Using style sheets, you
```

```
can keep your <abbr>CSS</abbr> presentation layer
and <abbr>HTML</abbr> content layer separate. This
is called "separation of concerns."</p>

</body>
</html>
```

Paragraph tag

You can use CSS (Cascading Style Sheets) to style your HTML (HyperText Markup Language).
Using style sheets, you can keep your CSS presentation layer and HTML content layer separate. This is called "separation of concerns."

Tag <p>.

The <b> <b> element is used to draw the reader's attention to the content of an element that is otherwise given no particular meaning. This was known as the Boldface element, and the most browsers draw text in bold. However, you cannot use <b> to style text; instead, you should use the CSS font-weight property to make the text bold, or the strong element to indicate that the text has special importance.

Example:

```
<!DOCTYPE html>
<html>
<head>
<style>
div {
   list-style-type: none;
   margin: 0;
   padding: 0px;
   overflow: hidden;
}

li {
   float: left;
     border-right: 1px solid black;
     color:black;
}

li a {
   display: block;
```

```
  font-size:20px;
   text-align: center;
   padding: 10px 20px;
   text-decoration: none;
   color:black;

}

</style>
</head>
<body>


<header>
    <h2> Normal text   </h2>
    <div>
        <li><a class="active" href="#home">Home</
a></li>
        <li><a href="#">Java</a></li>
        <li><a href="#">HTML</a></li>
        <li><a href="#">CSS</a></li>
      </div>

      <h2> Bold tag </h2>
    <div>
        <li><a class="active" href="#home"> <b>
Home </b></a></li>
        <li><a href="#">  <b> Java </b></a></li>
        <li><a href="#">  <b> HTML </b> </a></li>
        <li><a href="#">  <b> CSS </b> </a></li>
      </div>
   </header>

</body>
</html>
```

Normal text

Home | Java | HTML | CSS |

Bold tag

Home | **Java** | **HTML** | **CSS** |

Tag <b>.

<em> The <em> HTML element indicates text that is highlighted. The <em> element can nest, with each level of nesting indicating a greater degree of emphasis.

Example:

```
<!DOCTYPE html>
<html>
<head>
<style>
body{
  padding:10px;
  width:400px;
  margin:0 auto;
}
h1{
  text-align: center;
}
em{
  border-bottom: 1px solid green;
}

</style>
</head>
<body>
  <h1> p tag </h1>
    <p>
      Curabitur lacinia lectus ut quam tincidunt,
<em>Lorem</em> sit amet commodo dolor pharetra.
Curabitur lacinia lectus ut quam tincidunt, sit
amet commodo dolor pharetra.
    </p>

</body>
</html>
```

p tag

Curabitur lacinia lectus ut quam tincidunt, *Lorem* sit amet commodo dolor pharetra.Curabitur lacinia lectus ut quam tincidunt, sit amet commodo dolor pharetra.

Tag <em>.

The <i> <i> HTML element represents a range of text that differs from normal text for some reason, such as text, technical terms, taxonomic labels, among others. Historically, this data was shown in italics, which is the original source of the <i> naming of this element.

Example:

```
<!DOCTYPE html>
<html>
<head>
<style>
body{
   padding:10px;
   width:400px;
   margin:0 auto;
}
h1{
   text-align: center;
}
em{
   border-bottom: 1px solid green;
}

</style>
</head>
<body>
   <h1> i tag </h1>
     <i>
       Curabitur lacinia lectus ut quam tincidunt,
Lorem sit amet commodo dolor pharetra.Curabitur
lacinia lectus ut quam tincidunt, sit amet commodo
dolor pharetra.
   </i>

</body>
</html>
```

Curabitur lacinia lectus ut quam tincidunt, Lorem sit amet commodo dolor pharetra.Curabitur lacinia lectus ut quam tincidunt, sit amet commodo dolor pharetra.

Tag <em>.

<q> The <q> element indicates that the attached text is a short-embedded citation. Most modern browsers are implemented by surrounding the text with quotation marks. This element is intended for short citations that do not require paragraph breaks; use the blockquote element for long quotes.

```
<!DOCTYPE html>
<html>
<head>
<style>
body{
  padding:10px;
  width:400px;
  margin:0 auto;
}
h1{
  text-align: center;
}
em{
  border-bottom: 1px solid green;
}

</style>
</head>
<body>
  <h1> q tag </h1>
  <p>Inspirational Quotes : <q>Keep smiling, because
life is a beautiful thing and there's so much to smile
about. </q></p>
</body>
</html>
```

q tag

Inspirational Quotes : "Keep smiling, because life is a beautiful thing and there's so much to smile about. "

Tag <q>.

<kbd> The <kbd> HTML element represents a range of embedded text indicating textual user input from a keyboard, voice note, or any other text input device. By convention, the user agent renders the content of the <kbd> element using its default monospaced font by default, although the HTML standard does not mandate this.

Example:

```
<!DOCTYPE html>
<html>
<head>
<style>
body{
    padding:10px;
    width:400px;
    margin:0 auto;
}
h1{
    text-align: center;
}
em{
    border-bottom: 1px solid green;
}

</style>
</head>
<body>
    <h1> kbd tag </h1>
    <p> Please press <kbd>Ctrl</kbd> + <kbd> C </
kbd>  to   copy any content. </p>
    <p> Please press <kbd>Ctrl</kbd> + <kbd> X </
kbd>  to   cut any content. </p>
    <p> Please press <kbd>Ctrl</kbd> + <kbd> V </
kbd>  to   paste any content. </p>
</body>
</html>
```

kbd tag

Please press Ctrl + C to copy any content .

Please press Ctrl + X to cut any content .

Please press Ctrl + V to paste any content .

Tag <kbd>.

<mark> The HTML <mark> element represents text that is marked or highlighted for reference or notation purposes because of the relevance or importance of the marked passage in the accompanying context.

Example:

```
<!DOCTYPE html>
<html>
<head>
<style>
body{
  padding:10px;
  width:400px;
  margin:0 auto;
}
h1{
  text-align: center;
}
em{
  border-bottom: 1px solid green;
}

</style>
</head>
<body>
  <h1> mark tag </h1>
<p> <mark> Lorem </mark> ipsum dolor sit amet,
consectetur adipiscing elit. Cras id tincidunt
dui. Fusce congue metus leo, vitae condimentum
purus malesuada vel.</p>
<p><mark> Lorem </mark> ipsum dolor sit amet,
consectetur adipiscing elit. Cras id tincidunt
dui. Fusce congue metus leo, vitae condimentum
purus malesuada vel.</p>
</body>
</html>
```

mark tag

Lorem ipsum dolor sit amet, consectetur adipiscing elit. Cras id tincidunt dui. Fusce congue metus leo, vitae condimentum purus malesuada vel.

Lorem ipsum dolor sit amet, consectetur adipiscing elit. Cras id tincidunt dui. Fusce congue metus leo, vitae condimentum purus malesuada vel.

Tag <mark>.

<time> The <time> element used to represents a specific time period. It can include a DateTime attribute to convert the data into a machine-readable format, allowing for search engine results or also custom features such as reminders.

Example:

```
<!DOCTYPE html>
<html>
<head>
<style>
body{
  padding:10px;
  width:400px;
  margin:0 auto;
}
h1{
  text-align: center;
}
em{
  border-bottom: 1px solid green;
}
.language{
  color:red;
  font-size:20px
}

</style>
</head>
<body>
  <h1> time tag  </h1>
  <p>We will be celebrating our 40th anniversary
on <time datetime="2018-07-07">July 7</time> in
London's Hyde Park.</p>
  <p>The show starts at <time
datetime="20:00">20:00</time> and you will be able
to enjoy the function for at least <time
datetime="PT2H30M">2h 30m</time>.</p>
  </body>
</html>
```

time tag

We will be celebrating our 40th anniversary on July 7 in London's Hyde Park.

The concert starts at 20:00 and you'll be able to enjoy the band for at least 2h 30m.

Tag <time>.

<span> The <span> element is an inline container for phrasing content that doesn't actually represent anything. It can use to group elements for styling elements (use the class or id attributes), or the attribute values such as lang. It should be used when no other semantic element is suitable. <span> is very similar to the div element, but the div element is a block-level element, whereas the <span> element is an inline element.

Example:

```
<!DOCTYPE html>
<html>
<head>
<style>
body{
   padding:10px;
   width:400px;
   margin:0 auto;
}
h1{
   text-align: center;
}
em{
   border-bottom: 1px solid green;
}
.language{
   color: red;
   font-size:20px
}

</style>
</head>
<body>
   <h1> span tag  </h1>
```

```
<p> There are various programming languages such
as
    <span class="language"> Python  </span>,
    <span class="language"> Java </span>,
    <span class="language"> JavaScript </span>,
    <span class="language"> Swift </span>,
    <span class="language"> C </span> etc.
  </p>
</body>
</html>
```

span tag

There are various programming languages such as Python , Java , JavaScript , Swift , C etc.

Tag <span>.

<strong> The <strong> element indicates that its content is of great importance, severity, or urgency. Browsers usually render content in bold.

Example:

```
<!DOCTYPE html>
<html>
<head>
<style>
body{
  padding:10px;
  width:400px;
  margin:0 auto;
}
h1{
  text-align: center;
}
em{
  border-bottom: 1px solid green;
}
.language{
  color:red;
  font-size:20px
}
```

```
</style>
</head>
<body>
  <h1> strong tag  </h1>
  <p>Normal Text - There are various programming
languages such as Python, Java, JavaScript, Swift,
C etc. </p>
  <strong> Strong Text - There are various
programming languages such as Python, Java,
JavaScript, Swift, C etc. </strong>
</body>
</html>
```

strong tag

Normal Text - There are various programming languages such as Python, Java, JavaScript, Swift, C etc.

Strong Text - There are various programming languages such as Python, Java, JavaScript, Swift, C etc.

Tag <strong>.

<sub> The HTML <sub> element specifies embedded text that should be displayed as a subscript for typographical reasons only. Subscripts are usually rendered with a reduced outline using smaller text.

Example:

```
<!DOCTYPE html>
<html>
<head>
<style>
body{
  padding:10px;
  width:400px;
  margin:0 auto;
}
h1{
  text-align: center;
}
em{
```

```
    border-bottom: 1px solid green;
}
.language{
    color:red;
    font-size:20px
}

</style>
</head>
<body>
    <h1> sub tag </h1>
    <p> Sub Script : H <sub> 2 </sub> O </p>
</body>
</html>
```

sub tag

Sub Script : H $_2$ O

Tag <sub>.

<sup> The HTML <sup> element specifies embedded text to be displayed as a superscript for typographical reasons only. Superscripts are usually rendered with a raised outline using smaller text.

Example:

```
<!DOCTYPE html>
<html>
<head>
<style>
body{
    padding:10px;
    width:400px;
    margin:0 auto;
}
h1{
    text-align: center;
}
em{
    border-bottom: 1px solid green;
}
```

```
.language{
   color:red;
   font-size:20px
}

</style>
</head>
<body>
   <h1> sup tag  </h1>
   <p> Super Script: (a+b) <sup> 2 </sup> </p>
</body>
</html>
```

sup tag

Super Script: (a+b) ^{2}

Tag <sup>.

<u> The <u> HTML element represents a range of inline text that should be rendered in a way that indicates it contains non-textual annotation. This is rendered as a simple solid underline by default but can be changed with CSS.

Example:

```
<!DOCTYPE html>
<html>
<head>
<style>
body{
   padding:10px;
   width:400px;
   margin:0 auto;
}
h1{
   text-align: center;
}
em{
   border-bottom: 1px solid green;
}
```

```
 .language{
   color:red;
   font-size:20px
}

</style>
</head>
<body>
   <h1> u tag  </h1>
   <p> Normal Text - There are various programming
languages such as Python, Java, JavaScript, Swift,
C etc. </p>
      <u> Underline Text - There are various
programming languages such as Python, Java,
JavaScript, Swift, C etc. </u>
   </body>
   </html>
```

u tag

Normal Text - There are various programming languages such as Python, Java, JavaScript, Swift, C etc.

Underline Text - There are various programming languages such as Python, Java, JavaScript, Swift, C etc.

Tag <u>.

TABLES

We use tables to display information that is presented in tabular form. The common use of tables is to control the layout of a page.

Most of the tables are made up of the following elements:

- <table> – The element containing all information about the table

- <tr> – the 'table row' element that defines a row

- <th> – the 'table heading' element that defines a heading cell

- <td> – the 'table data' element that defines a cell

- The <table> element should appear within the document's <body> element.

Example:

```
<html>
<head>
<title> Title <title>
 </head>
<body>
<!-- Some elements could appear here -->
<table>
    <tr>  <!-- Beginning of the 1st row -->
        <th> Row 1, column 1 </th> <!-- 1st
heading cell in this row -->
        <th> Row 1, column 2</th> <!-- 2nd
heading cell in this row -->
    </tr> <!-- End of the 1st row -->
    <tr>
        <td> Row 2, column 1 </td>
        <td> Row 2, column 2 </td>
    </tr>
    <tr>  <!-- Beginning of the 3rd row -->
        <td> Row 3, column 1 </td> <!-- 1st data
cell in this row -->
        <td>Row 3, column 2</td> <!-- 2nd data
cell in this row -->
    </tr>  <!-- End of the 3rd row -->
    <tr>
        <td> Row 4, column 1 </td>
        <td> Row 4, column 2 </td>
    </tr>
</table>
</body>
</html>
```

Table tag

Row 1, column 1 Row 1, column 2
Row 2, column 1 Row 2, column 2
Row 3, column 1 Row 3, column 2
Row 4, column 1 Row 4, column 2

Tag <table>.

OTHER INTERACTIVE ELEMENTS

HTML offers a selection of elements that help create interactive user interface objects.

<details> The HTML <details> element creates an accessibility widget in which information is only visible when the widget is switched to the "open" state. A label must be provided using the details element.

Syntax:

```
<details>
  <summary>  Text content  </summary>
  <div> Content. . .  >
</details>
```

Example:

```
<html>
<head>
<title> Title </title>
 </head>
<body>
  <h2> Details tag </h2>
  <details>
    <summary>  Front end Technology:  </summary>
        <div>  1. HTML (HyperText Markup Language)
</div>
        <div> 2. CSS (Cascading Style Sheets)
</div>
        <div> 3. JavaScript </div>
        <div> 4. React </div>
        <div> 5. Angular  </div>
        <div> 6. Vue  </div>
</details>
<details>
  <summary>  Back end Technology:  </summary>
      <div> 1. JavaScript </div>
      <div> 2. Python </div>
      <div> 3. Ruby </div>
      <div> 4. PHP </div>
      <div> 5. Java  </div>
      <div> 6. Scala  </div>
</details>
</body>
</html>
```

Details tag

▼ Front end Technology:
1. HTML (HyperText Markup Language)
2. CSS (Cascading Style Sheets)
3. JavaScript
4. React
5. Angular
6. Vue
▼ Back end Technology:
1. JavaScript
2. Python
3. Ruby
4. PHP
5. Java
6. Scala

tag <details>.

<dialog> The <dialog> element represents a dialog box or other component, such as a dismissable alert, inspector, or pane.

Example:

```
<html>
<head>
<title> Title </title>
 </head>
<body>
  <h2> dialog tag </h2>
  <div>
    <dialog id="DialogExample">
      <p>
        Here is some text for example.
      </p>
      <button id="hide">Close dialog text</button>
    </dialog>
    <button id="show">Show dialog text</button>
  </div>
  <script type="text/JavaScript">
    (function() { var dialog = document.getElement
ById('DialogExample'); document.
```

```
getElementById('show').onclick = function() {
dialog.show(); }; document.getElementById('hide').
onclick = function() { dialog.close(); }; })();
  </script>
</body>
</html>
```

dialog tag

| Show dialog text |

Here is some text for example.

| Close dialog text |

Tag <dialog>.

<summary> The HTML <summary> element specifies a summary, title, or legend for the disclosure field of the detail element. Clicking on the <summary> element toggles the open and closed state of the parent <details> element.

```
<html>
<head>
<title> Title </title>
 </head>
<body>
  <h2> Details tag </h2>
  <details>
    <summary>  Front end Technology:  </summary>
        <div>  1. HTML (HyperText Markup Language)
</div>
        <div> 2. CSS (Cascading Style Sheets) </div>
        <div> 3. JavaScript </div>
        <div> 4. React </div>
        <div> 5. Angular  </div>
        <div> 6. Vue  </div>
</details>
<details>
  <summary>  Back end Technology:  </summary>
      <div> 1. JavaScript </div>
      <div> 2. Python </div>
```

```
      <div> 3. Ruby </div>
      <div> 4. PHP </div>
      <div> 5. Java  </div>
      <div> 6. Scala  </div>
</details>
</body>
</html>
```

HTML CHARACTER ESCAPE

In HTML, escape characters can be used to represent any Unicode character using only ASCII characters. Character escapes used in markup include numeric characters and named character references. You can use numeric or named character references, and CSS escapes to represent characters in HTML style attributes.

In the following you can find the complete list of the useful HTML escape characters in order:[30]

- Lower Case Alphabets

- Upper Case Alphabets

- Numeric Value

- Other Various Symbols

Lower Case Alphabets

ASCII Number		Sign	Name	Explanation
97	a	a	&#97;	Lowercase
98	b	b	&#98;	Lowercase
99	c	c	&#99;	Lowercase
100	d	d	&#100;	Lowercase
101	e	e	&#101;	Lowercase
102	f	f	&#102;	Lowercase
103	g	g	&#103;	Lowercase
104	h	h	&#104;	Lowercase
105	i	i	&#105;	Lowercase
106	j	j	&#106;	Lowercase
107	k	k	&#107;	Lowercase
108	l	l	&#108;	Lowercase
109	m	m	&#109;	Lowercase
110	n	n	&#110;	Lowercase

(Continued)

ASCII Number	Sign	Name	Explanation
111 o	o	&#111;	Lowercase
112 p	p	&#112;	Lowercase
113 q	q	&#113;	Lowercase
114 r	r	&#114;	Lowercase
115 s	s	&#115;	Lowercase
116 t	t	&#116;	Lowercase
117 u	u	&#117;	Lowercase
118 v	v	&#118;	Lowercase
119 w	w	&#119;	Lowercase
120 x	x	&#120;	Lowercase
121 y	y	&#121;	Lowercase
122 z	z	&#122;	Lowercase

Upper Case Alphabets

65 A	A	&#65;	Uppercase
66 B	B	&#66;	Uppercase
67 C	C	&#67;	Uppercase
68 D	D	&#68;	Uppercase
69 E	E	&#69;	Uppercase
70 F	F	&#70;	Uppercase
71 G	G	&#71;	Uppercase
72 H	H	&#72;	Uppercase
73 I	I	&#73;	Uppercase
74 J	J	&#74;	Uppercase
75 K	K	&#75;	Uppercase
76 L	L	&#76;	Uppercase
77 M	M	&#77;	Uppercase
78 N	N	&#78;	Uppercase
79 O	O	&#79;	Uppercase
80 P	P	&#80;	Uppercase
81 Q	Q	&#81;	Uppercase
82 R	R	&#82;	Uppercase
83 S	S	&#83;	Uppercase
84 T	T	&#84;	Uppercase
85 U	U	&#85;	Uppercase
86 V	V	&#86;	Uppercase
87 W	W	&#87;	Uppercase
88 X	X	&#88;	Uppercase
89 Y	Y	&#89;	Uppercase
90 Z	Z	&#90;	Uppercase

Numeric Value

49	1	&#49;	Digit 1
50	2	&#50;	Digit 2
51	3	&#51;	Digit 3
52	4	&#52;	Digit 4
53	5	&#53;	Digit 5
54	6	&#54;	Digit 6
55	7	&#55;	Digit 7
56	8	&#56;	Digit 8
57	9	&#57;	Digit 9

Other Symbols

ASCII Number	Sign	Name	Code
9	Tab	&Tab;	&#9;
10	New Line	&NewLine;	&#10;
32	Space		&#32;
33	!	&#33;	Exclamation mark
34	"	&quot;	&#34;
35	#	&#35;	Number sign
36	$	&#36;	Dollar sign
37	%	&#37;	Percent sign
38	&	&amp;	& Ampersand
39	'	&#39;	Apostrophe
40	(	&#40;	Opening/Left parenthesis
41	)	&#41;	Closing/Right parenthesis
42	*	&#42;	Asterisk
43	+	&#43;	Plus sign
44	,	&#44;	Comma
45	–	&#45;	Hyphen
46	.	&#46;	Period
47	/	&#47;	Slash
58	:	&#58;	Colon
59	;	&#59;	Semicolon
60	<	< (<)	Less-than
61	=	&#61;	Equals sign
62	>	> (>)	Greater than
63	?	&#63;	Question mark
64	@	&#64;	At sign
91	[	&#91;	Opening/Left square bracket
92	\	&#92;	Backslash
93	]	&#93;	Closing/Right square bracket
94	^	&#94;	Caret
95	_	&#95;	Underscore
96	`	&#96;	Grave accent

(Continued)

ASCII Number	Sign	Name	Code	
123	{	&#123;		Opening/Left curly brace
124	|	|		Vertical bar
125	}	&#125;		Closing/Right curly brace
126	~	&#126;		Tilde
128	€	&#128;		Euro sign
130	,	&#130;		Punctuation mark
177	±	± (±)		Plus or minus

TEXT FORMATTING TAGS

HTML formatting is a process that allows formatting Text to increase its visual appeal.[31] Various HTML tags can change the appearance of Text on a web page and make the Text attractive. We can use text formatting tags for bold, italics, underline, and more.

The following example shows the commonly used HTML formatting tags. Now try to understand how these tags actually work.

- <small>
- <tt>
- <u>
- <b>
- <strong>
- <i>
- <em>
- <mark>
- <sup>
- <del>
- <ins>
- <strie>
- <big>
- <sub>
- <small>
- <big>

The below table will tell the basic definition of the formatting tags.

HTML Text Formatting Tag	Description
<b>	It specifies bold text
<strong>	It works same as the <b> tag but denotes important text
<i>	It defines italics text
<em>	It specifies the emphasized text
<mark>	It defines highlighted text
<sup>	It shows superscripted text
<sub>	It shows subscripted text
<small>	It is used to specify text with a smaller font size
<big>	It is used to specify text with a larger font size
<del>	It is used to define deleted text
<ins>	It is used to define inserted text
<strike>	It is used to draw a strikethrough on a section of text. But it is not supported in HTML5
<big>	It increases the font size by one conventional unit
<small> .	It decreases the font size by one unit from the base font size
<u>	It is used to underline text written between it
<tt>	It is used to appear as a text in teletype. But it is not supported in HTML5

HTML PHRASE TAG

The HTML phrase tags are special tags, which define the structural meaning of a block of text or semantics of text.[32] The following is the list of phrase tags, some of which we have already discussed in HTML formatting above.

- Abbreviation tag: <abbr>

- Acronym tag: <acronym>

- Definition tag: <dfn>

- Quoting tag: <blockquote>

- Short quote tag: <q>

- Code tag: <code>

- Keyboard tag: <kbd>

- Address tag: <address>

HTML FORMS

Forms offer controls for almost every application use. Using form controls and fields, we can request small and large amounts of information such as user ID, password, billing details, job application, etc. You create and modify the form and its elements by resetting styles using the appearance property, setting consistent style for the form, adding placeholder responses for text fields, and customizing radio buttons and checkboxes using various pseudo-classes and pseudo-elements.

Now first setup the basic HTML and CSS code for forms then save the file with index.html page. Begin by opening the index.html file in any coding editor. Then, add the following HTML code to provide a base structure for the file.

```
<!doctype html>
<html>
  <head>
    <meta charset="utf-8">
    <meta content="width=device-width,
name="viewport" initial-scale=1">
    <title>CSS Form</title>
    <link rel="stylesheet" href="styles.css" />
  </head>
  <body>
    <main>

  Add your code here.

    </main>
  </body>
</html>
```

The elements contained in the <head> tag define the title of the page with the <title> tag where to load the stylesheet using the <link> tag. <meta> tags define the character encoding and guide the browser on how to display the website on a small-screen device. The content of the form will be placed inside the <body> and <main> tags.

Next, in the <main> tag, create a <form> element. Inside the <form> tag, add various form elements and <div> elements to help with the layout. This tutorial highlights the additions to the code from the previous steps. Add the highlighted HTML from the following block of code to the index.html file.

BASIC STRUCTURE OF FORMS

In order to get information through a form, we must first learn how to create it.[33]

Syntax:

```
<form action="URL" method="post">
    /* form inputs*/
    </form>
```

To add a form to a web page, we need to add a <form> tag. All input fields and form controls should be wrapped in a <form> element. There are many attributes available for a form element, but the most used or important ones are action and method.

HTML – TEXT LINKS

The website may contain various links that take you directly to other pages and even to specific parts of the page.[34] These links are known as hyperlinks. It allows users to navigate between websites by clicking on words, phrases, and images. It allows you to create hyperlinks using text or images available on a web page.

The link is specified using the HTML <a> tag. This tag is called an anchor tag, and anything between the opening <a> tag and the close.

HTML IMAGES

Images enhance the appearance of the web pages by creating them more interesting and colorful. The <img> elements are used to insert images in the documents. It is an empty element that contains attributes only. The syntax of the <img> tag can be given below.

The following example adds three images on the web page:

```
<html>
<head>
<link rel="shortcut icon" href="favicon.ico"
type="image/x-icon">
</head>
<title> Example of favicon </title>
<body>
```

```
<img src="https://images.pexels.com/photos/13146110/
pexels-photo-13146110.jpeg?auto=compress&cs=tinysrgb&w
=300&lazy=load" alt=" Bird ">
</body>
</html>
```

Each image carries at least two attributes such as the src attribute and an alt attribute. The attribute src tells the browser where to find the image and its value is the URL of the image file. Whereas, the alt attribute provides a text for the image if it cannot be displayed for some reason because when the browser gets the path the image will show otherwise the alt value will show. Its value must be a meaningful content for the image.

Also, the <img> tag has other various tags such as width and height of an image. Both width and height attributes are used to specify the width and height of an image.

```
<html>
<head>
<link rel="shortcut icon" href="favicon.ico"
type="image/x-icon">
</head>
<title> Example of favicon </title>
<body>
  <img src="https://images.pexels.com/photos/13146110/
pexels-photo-13146110.jpeg?auto=compress&cs=tinysrgbw=
300&lazy=load" alt=" Bird " width="300" height="300">
</body>
</html>
```

HTML iFRAMES

An iframe tag is used to display a nested web page (a web page within a web page). The HTML <iframe> element defines an inline frame, that's why it's also called an inline frame. An iframe works like a mini web browser inside a web browser. Also, the content inside the iframe element exists completely independently of the surrounding elements.

An HTML iframe tag is defined with the <iframe> tag the syntax is given below.

```
<iframe src="URL"> </iframe>
```

Example:

```
<!DOCTYPE html>
<html>
<head>
<style>
body{
  padding:10px;
  width:400px;
  margin:0 auto;
}
h1{
  text-align: center;
}

#example-paragraphs {
  background-color: grey;
  overflow: hidden;
  resize: horizontal;
  width: 9rem;
}

</style>
</head>
<body>
  <h2> HTML Iframes </h2>
  <p> Not using the height and width attributes
</p>
  <iframe src="https://www.google.com/" >
</iframe>
  <p> Using the height and width attributes</p>
  <iframe src="https://www.google.com/"
height="300" width="400"> </iframe>
</body>
</html>
```

HTML Iframes

Not using the height and width attributes

Using the height and width attributes

Tag <iframe>.

You can set the width and height of the iframe by using "width" & "height" attributes. The attribute values are specified in pixels by default, but you can also set them in percentages like 50%, 60%, etc.

HTML – EMBED MULTIMEDIA

Embedding Multimedia in HTML is adding images, audio, video, and other plugins to the web using special HTML tags, the web browser started to support text and colors.[35] Multimedia has interactive content. Let's understand HTML Embed Multimedia in detail.

Embedded Multimedia

Multimedia elements are embedded in the documents by various methods, which are also used to add media files to an HTML web page supported by various types and formats.

There are three ways to add multimedia to the web page.

The <embed> Tag

The <embed> tag is used to add multimedia files of external applications, which are mainly audio and video, and other plugins to a web page.

- <embed> tag: Supported by most web browsers and new in HTML5.

- <embed> tag: It only has an opening tag and does not guarantee to have a closing tag.

- <noembed> tag: Used when no web browser recognizes the HTML <embed> tag.

Syntax:

```
<embed src="URL">
```

The source (src) attribute is used to embed media into a document with the <embed> tag, and various media types are supported in <embed> elements.

Example:

```
<!DOCTYPE html>
<html>
<head>
<style>
body{
  padding:10px;
  width:400px;
  margin:0 auto;
}
h1{
  text-align: center;
}
table {
  font-family: Arial, sans-serif;
  width: 100%;
}

td, the {
  border: 1px solid black;
  text-align: left;
```

```
    padding: 8px;
}

tr:nth-child(even) {
    background-color: #dddddd;
}
</style>

</head>
<body>
    <h2> HTML Embeded Multimedia ( embed tag )</h2>
    <embed src="https://images.pexels.com/
photos/1781932/pexels-photo-1781932.jpeg?auto=comp
ress&cs=tinysrgb&w=400&lazy=load" height="400"
width="400"> </embed>
    </body>
</html>
```

HTML Embeded Multimedia (embed tag)

Tag <embed>.

The <bgsound> Tag

You can use the <bgsound> HTML tag to play an audio track in the background of your web page. Only Internet Explorer supports this tag, and most other browsers ignore this tag. When a user first downloads and displays a host document, it downloads and plays an audio file. The background audio file will also play whenever the user refreshes the browser.

Points to remember:

- The <bgsound> tag in an HTML document is used to add background sound media to a web page.

- <bgsound> tag: Mainly used in Internet Explorer and ignored by most browsers. It is deprecated from the latest version of HTML.

- <bgsound> tag: Used when playing background sound repeatedly whenever the browser refreshes the HTML document.

- <audio> tag: Used in the latest version of HTML instead of the <bgsound> tag.

- <bgsound> tag: It does not display any content, only the accompanying sound in the HTML document.

There are two main attributes used in the <bgsound> element to add background sound.

- loop – Defines how many times the background sound will be played in a loop with specified conditions.

- src – Defines the URL path to the embedded audio track.

HTML <object> Tag

HTML 4 introduces the <object> element, which offers a universal solution for embedding generic objects. The <object> element allows HTML authors to specify everything an object requires to be presented by a user agent. The <object> tag is used to add external object multimedia files, which are mainly audio, images, pdf, flash, video, and other web pages to the current web page.

- The <object> tag is supported by web browsers. It was introduced in HTML 4.

- The <object> element is defined in the <body> tag of an HTML document.

- The <param> tag is used as plugin parameters that have been included with the <object> tag.

- An HTML document object can be defined under the <object> tag of the current HTML document.

Here is the syntax of the object

```
<object type=""> </object> or <object data="">
</object>
```

- Attributes of the <object> tag: Common attributes used in the <object> element to add multimedia to HTML are as follows:

  - height: It defines the height of the multimedia object in pixels.

  - form: It defines the form ID of the object element.

  - width: It defines the width of the multimedia object in pixels.

  - type: It defines the media type of the embedded plug-in.

HTML MARQUEE

The Marquee Element in HTML is used to handle the effect of scrolling text and images in different directions using attributes on a web page of an HTML document to improve the appearance of the web.[36]

Usage

The HTML <marquee> tag is a container tag used to define the scrolling effect of a text or image element vertically or horizontally, or more precisely, the scrolling of the element is either top to bottom or vice versa or left to right or vice versa.

The <marquee> tag supports global and event attributes and is only supported by a few browsers, e.g. firefox, Internet explorer, safari, chrome, etc. A marquee tag starts with an opening tag and ends with a closing tag with the attribute value and content in between.

Syntax:

```
<marquee attribute name = "marquee attribute
value..."> content </marquee>
```

Example:

```
<!DOCTYPE html>
<html>
<head>
<style>
body{
   padding:10px;
   width:680px;
   margin:0 auto;
}
h1{
   text-align: center;
}
p{
   font-size:20px
}
</style>

</head>
<embed>
   <h1> HTML Marquee tag </h1>
   <marquee> <p> Lorem ipsum dolor sit amet,
consectetur adipiscing elit. In viverra nunc non
diam faucibus, non cursus metus elementum.
Vestibulum vel sapien sapien. Ut a est viverra,
tempus metus sed, lacinia mi. Suspendisse potenti.
</p> </marquee>
</body>
</html>
```

The output of the above mentioned code is given below.

HTML Marquee tag

Lorem ipsum dolor sit amet, consectetur adipiscing elit. In viverra m

Tag <marquee>.

ATTRIBUTES IN <marquee> TAG

There are various attributes of <marquee> tag in HTML as given below:

Attributes	Description
behavior	The attribute is used to define the type of scrolling in the frame with values like slide, scroll, and alternative.
Direction	This attribute is used to define the scrolling direction with a value of up, down, right, and left.
width	The attribute is used to define the width of the selection in pixels or percentages.
height	The attribute is used to define the height of the selection in pixels or percentages.
scroll delay	The attribute is used to define the delay between scrolls in milliseconds.
scroll amount	The attribute is used to define an interval in the selection speed in numbers.
Loop	The attribute is used to define the number of times to scroll the frame in number, the default number is infinite.
Vspace	The attribute is used to define the vertical space around the frame with a value in pixels.
Hspace	The attribute is used to define the horizontal space around the frame with a value in pixels.

HTML Properties

Before delving into this full HTML book, there are some basics that need to be clarified. As a beginner, you should be aware of HTML properties and features. Only then can you be interested in HTML programming. Let's discuss some important properties of HTML.

- Develop website structure. All blocks and elements on the web exist because there is HTML.

- Simple, human-readable tags represent elements on web pages. Therefore, they are easy to remember.

- Widely supported by all browsers. It is a markup language for web development.

- HTML5 can help improve your gaming experience.

- Easy to learn and implement.

- It is platform-independent and works on all operating systems.

BENEFITS

- HTML is very easy to learn and understand. HTML is the first and most important language for anyone learning web development. Simple markup, HTML is not case-sensitive.

- There are only a few markings that serve the purpose. You don't have much to understand, so you can easily understand other people's code and modify it as needed. Moreover, if the developer forgets to close the tag or makes some mistakes in the code, it will not cause any errors or problems like in other programming languages.

- One of the biggest advantages of HTML is that it's free and doesn't require you to buy any special software.

- HTML is supported by almost all browsers. HTML gives web developers an easy way to optimize website in HTML depending on the browser.

- HTML is one of the most search engine-friendly languages compared to all other programming languages available in the market.

CHAPTER SUMMARY

This chapter is all about brief explanations of HTML fundamentals such as the tools and editor used to write code in HTML. Also, we write some simple code using class, id, and internal and external CSS. We will also explain the properties, features, and more in the following chapters.

NOTES

1. Frontend and backend Technology – https://www.altexsoft.com/blog/frontend-development-technologies-concepts/, accessed on August 31, 2022.
2. How HTML Works – https://www.altexsoft.com/blog/front-end-development-technologies-concepts/, accessed on August 31, 2022.
3. CSS Works – https://www.altexsoft.com/blog/front-end-development-technologies-concepts/, accessed on August 31, 2022.
4. HTML DOM – https://www.altexsoft.com/blog/front-end-development-technologies-concepts/, accessed on August 31, 2022.
5. DOM – https://www.w3.org/TR/WD-DOM/introduction.html, accessed on August 31, 2022.
6. JavaScript – https://www.altexsoft.com/blog/front-end-development-technologies-concepts/, accessed on August 31, 2022.
7. HTML Markup Language – https://www.thoughtco.com/what-are-markup-languages-3468655, accessed on August 31, 2022.

8. HTML – https://en.wikipedia.org/wiki/HTML#History/, accessed on August 31, 2022.

9. HTML History – History – https://www.washington.edu/accesscomputing/webd2/student/unit1/module3/html_history.html#:~:text=The%20first%20version%20of%20HTML,HTML%20as%20an%20XML%20language./, accessed on August 31, 2022.

10. HTML History – https://en.wikipedia.org/wiki/HTML#History/, accessed on August 31, 2022.

11. HTML Version – https://www.tutorialstonight.com/html/history-of-html, accessed on September 9, 2022.

12. HTML Version list – https://www.howtocodeschool.com/2019/01/html-versions.html#HTML-2.0, accessed on September 1, 2022.

13. XHTML – https://www.geeksforgeeks.org/difference-between-xhtml-and-html5/#:~:text=XHTML%20stands%20for%20Extensible%20Hypertext, a%20better%20version%20of%20HTML, accessed on September 1, 2022.

14. HTML Structure – https://www.w3docs.com/learn-html/html-introduction.html/, accessed on September 3, 2022.

15. HTML Basic Concepts – https://www.w3docs.com/learn-html/html-introduction.html Accessed on, accessed on September 1, 2022.

16. HTML Tags – https://www.coderepublics.com/HTML/html-tags.php/, accessed on September 1, 2022.

17. HTML image tag – https://www.coderepublics.com/HTML/html-tags.php/, accessed on September 1, 2022.

18. HTML Structure Tag – https://itwebtutorials.mga.edu/html/chp2/document-structure.aspx, accessed on September 2, 2022.

19. HTML Tags List – https://way2tutorial.com/html/tag/index.php, accessed on September 1, 2022; HTML Structure – https://www.w3docs.com/learn-html/html-introduction.html, accessed on September 1, 2022.

20. HTML Editor and Tools – https://www.w3docs.com/learn-html/html-editors.html accessed/, accessed on September 3, 2022.

21. HTML Comments – https://data-flair.training/blogs/html-comments/, accessed on September 3, 2022.

22. Tags and Elements – https://www.scaler.com/topics/difference-between-html-elements-and-tags/, accessed on September 3, 2022.

23. HTML Elements – https://mundrisoft.com/tech-bytes/types-of-html-elements-and-tags/, accessed on September 3, 2022.

24. HTML Elements – https://www.javatpoint.com/html-elements, accessed on September 3, 2022.

25. HTML Elements – https://www.naukri.com/learning/articles/html-elements/, accessed on September 3, 2022.

26. HTML Attributes – https://www.w3.org/TR/2010/WD-html-markup-20101019/syntax.html, accessed on September 3, 2022.

27. Attributes List – https://developer.mozilla.org/en-US/docs/Web/HTML/Attributes#attribute_list, accessed on September 3, 2022.

28. HTML Common Attributes – https://www.tutorialrepublic.com/html-tutorial/html-attributes.php, accessed on September 3, 2022.

29. HTML Structure – https://developer.mozilla.org/en-US/docs/Learn/Getting_started_with_the_web/HTML_basics#anatomy_of_an_html_element, accessed on September 4, 2022.
30. HTML Entities – https://mateam.net/html-escape-characters/, accessed on September 3, 2022.
31. HTML Formatting Tags – https://www.javatpoint.com/html-formatting, accessed on September 11, 2022.
32. HTML Phrases – https://www.w3schools.in/html/phrase-tags, accessed on September 16, 2022.
33. HTML Forms – https://www.studytonight.com/cascading-style-sheet/css-forms, accessed on September 17, 2022.
34. HTML Links – https://www.tutorialspoint.com/html/html_text_links.htm#, accessed on September 11, 2022.
35. HTML Multimedia – https://www.tutorialspoint.com/html/html_embed_multimedia.htm, accessed on September 16, 2022.
36. HTML Marquee – https://codedec.com/tutorials/marquee-tag-in-html/, accessed on September 16, 2022.

HTML Basic Usage

IN THIS CHAPTER

- ➤ Introduction HTML basic
- ➤ Script and Dynamic element
- ➤ Correlation with Js and CSS
- ➤ DOM in HTML

In the previous chapter, we covered the fundamental of the HTML. Now, here you will get all the basic information of HTML separately such as all the tags and elements in separate sections so that you will get to know why all these are used in HTML.

This section of the chapter introduces the concepts of web scripting and the JavaScript language. As you progress through the lessons, you will learn how to insert JavaScript commands directly into the HTML document, and how the script executes when you view the page in your browser. It works with a simple script, edits it, and tests it in browser while learning the basic tasks involved in creating and using JavaScript scripts.

INTRODUCTION

The first browsers didn't support images on web pages. The web has come in a long way since its early days. In addition to useful content, the website nowadays is rich in visual and interactive features such as graphics, sound, animation, and video. Using a web scripting language like JavaScript is

DOI: 10.1201/9781003357537-2

one of the easiest ways to upgrade any web pages and interact with users in new interactive ways.

LEARNING WEB SCRIPTING BASICS

You already know how to use two languages: HTML and Cascading Style Sheet (CSS) in the previous chapter.[1] You can use HTML tags to describe how the document should be formatted. CSS is then used to describe how the document should be displayed, and the browser will display the decorated content to the user. However, HTML and CSS are simple text-based languages and cannot respond to users, make decisions, or automate repetitive tasks. Such interactive tasks require more sophisticated languages: programming or scripting languages.

Many programming languages are complex, but scripting languages are generally simple. They have a simple syntax, perform tasks with minimal commands, and are easy to learn. JavaScript is a web scripting language that allows scripts to be combined with HTML and CSS to create interactive web pages.

SCRIPTING LANGUAGES VS. PROGRAMMING LANGUAGES

Essentially all scripting languages are programming languages. The theoretical difference between scripting languages and programming languages is that scripting languages do not require a compilation process but are instead interpreted. For example, C programs typically need to be compiled before they can be run, whereas scripting languages such as JavaScript and PHP typically don't.

Compiled programs generally run faster than interpreted programs because they are first converted to native machine code. Also, the compiler reads and analyzes the code only once and reports the errors in the code collectively, whereas the interpreter reads and analyzes the statements in the code as they are encountered and returns the field and stop.

SCRIPTING LANGUAGES

Scripting languages are usually interpreted.[2] The main purpose of scripting languages is not to build applications, but to provide behavior to existing applications. It is used to write code that can point to a software system. You can automate processes in your software system. A written script is essentially a set of instructions to a software system. The scripting language has evolved into a powerful language. We are no longer limited to writing small scripts to automate operations on software systems. You can also create rich applications using scripting languages. You can manipulate, customize, and automate the installation of existing systems. Useful functions are already available through the interface. Scripting languages provide a way for exposing program control functions.

WHY DO WE NEED SCRIPTING LANGUAGES?

Scripting languages interpret scripts only while the program is running.[3] Scripts are used to improve performance or perform common application tasks. Scripting languages are:

- Perl

- PHP

- JavaScript

- Python etc.

Server-side scripts (such as PHP) are interpreted on the server and client-side scripts (JavaScript) are executed by the client application.

SCRIPT

Web scripts provide the same type of instructions to web browsers. JavaScript scripts can range from a single line to an entire application. (In both cases, JavaScript scripts are typically run in a browser.)

Some programming languages must be compiled or converted to machine code before they can be run. JavaScript, on the other side, is an interpreted language. Any browser executes each line of script as it comes.

Interpreted languages have one big advantage. It is very easy to write or modify scripts. Modifying a JavaScript script is as easy as modifying a regular HTML document and changes take effect as soon as you reload the document in your browser.

WEB SCRIPTS AND THEIR TYPES

The process of creating scripts and embedding them in web pages is called web scripting.[4] A script or computer script is a list of commands, usually embedded in a web page, interpreted and executed by a specific program or scripting engine.

- Scripts can be created for a variety of purposes. Automating processes or generating web pages on your local computer.

- The programming languages in which scripts are written are called scripting languages, and there are many scripting languages today.

- Common scripting languages include VBScript, JavaScript, ASP, PHP, PERL, and JSP.

TYPES OF SCRIPTS

There are two main types of scripts. Client-side scripts are first downloaded on the client-side, then interpreted and executed by the browser (the system's default browser).

- Client-side scripts are browser dependent. In other words, the client-side browser must be scriptable in order to execute scripts.

- Here are some popular client-side scripting languages such as VBScript, JavaScript, and Hypertext Processor (PHP).

- When using client-side interactions, client-side scripts are used. Some examples of client-side script usage include the following.

Server-side Scripts

- Server-side scripts complete or perform tasks on the server side and send the results to the client side.

- With server-side scripting, the server does all the work, so it doesn't matter which browser you use on the client side.

- Server-side scripts are primarily used when information is sent to the server and processed on the server side.

DYNAMIC ELEMENTS

A dynamic element is an HTML element created by JavaScript code after the page loads.[5] Dynamic elements can be clicked and selected like any other element on the page. For example, the JavaScript code that displays the modal box creates element to darken the background of the modal box.

Dynamic HTML is a collective term for a combination of HTML tags and options that make web pages more animated and interactive than previous versions of HTML. Much of dynamic HTML is specified in HTML 4.0.

Simple examples of dynamic HTML features include text headings that change color when the user mouse over them and the ability for users to "drag and drop" images elsewhere on their web page. Dynamic HTML allows web documents to look and function like desktop applications and multimedia productions.

Features in Dynamic HTML

- An object-oriented view of a web page with its elements

- CSSs and the layering of content

- Dynamic fonts

AN OBJECT-ORIENTED VIEW

Each page element (such as division or section, heading, paragraph, image, list, and so forth) is viewed as an "object". For example, each heading on a page can be named, given attributes of text style and color, and addressed by name in a small program called "script" that is included on the page. The heading or any other element on the page can be changed as the result of a specified event such as a mouse passing over or being clicked or a time elapsing or an image can move from one place to another by "dragging and dropping" the image object with the mouse. Any change takes place immediately. Thus, variations can be thought of as different properties of the object.

Element variations can change the wording and color of the text, as well as replace everything contained in the Heading object with new content containing different or additional HTML code and text.

JavaScript controls have existed in previous layers of web pages, but dynamic HTML makes programming on web pages easier because a single program can handle more elements of the page.

A feature called dynamic fonts allows web page designers to include font files with specific font styles, sizes, and colors as part of a web page, and download the fonts with the page.

STYLESHEETS AND LAYERING

A stylesheet describes the standard style characteristics of a document or part of a document, including page layout, font styles, and size of text elements such as headings and bodies. For web pages, stylesheets also describe the default background color or image, the color of hypertext links, and sometimes the content of the page. Stylesheets help ensure consistency across all pages or groups of pages within a document or website.

It includes the ability to specify stylesheets in a "cascading style sheet" manner. As a result of user interaction, new stylesheets can be applied to change the appearance of the web page. You can have multiple levels of stylesheets on your page. A new stylesheet may differ from the stylesheet above it in only one element.

Layering is the use of alternate stylesheets or other approaches to modify the content of a page by providing layers of content that can overlay existing sections of content. Layers can be programmed to appear as part of a timed presentation or as a result of user interaction.

CORRELATION WITH CSS AND JS

Here we will discuss the relationship between CSS, JavaScript, and HTML.[6] All these files should be presented in the same folder because each of these three languages serves a different purpose, web developers typically use separate files for each. This idea is called "separation of concerns" and each file should have a different function across the website. Technically he could put all the code in one HTML file, but as the site scales it will eventually lead to code repetition.

Let's have a look at the code needed to create a complete house. All three files must be in the same directory (folder on your computer). In our home folder, we have files of each type. Name your main HTML file index, main CSS file style, and main JavaScript file script.

Every HTML file has three separate sections:

- The <head> in <title>, where you can include metadata and links to services like Google Fonts, Bootstrap files (.css).

- The <body>, where you include the actual HTML elements.

- The <script> tags under <body>, which can link to JavaScript files (.js).

Example:

```
<html>
    <head>
        <link rel="stylesheet" type="stylesheet">
    </head>
```

```
    <body>
        <h1> Write you content here </h1>
        <script src="script.js"> </script>
    </body>
</html>
```

HTML is at the core part of every web page, regardless of the complexity of the website or the number of technologies involved.[7] This is a basic skill for all web professionals. This is the starting point for anyone learning how to create content for the web. Fortunately, learning is surprisingly easy.

How Does HTML Work?

All HTML files contain many nested elements along with tags.[8] Most people can create a .html file with a simple text editor, upload it to the internet, and start creating their own web page. Additionally, Web data servers need to know how to handle uploaded files and how to send files to client computers for understanding. HTML code is used for this. It's the glue that holds everything together. HTML pages contain many elements that are fortunately easy to understand because they have names that describe what they are (i.e. header tags, paragraph tags, image tags).

All websites consist of these tags. Next, you neatly wrap the plain text content of your website (what you want your users to see) with a series of tags that tell the page what kind of content it is. This allows web browsers to understand how each content type will look in the HTML file. The Paragraph tag divides the content into neat little paragraphs, and the Header tag arranges the words on the page like a proper heading. You should start the tag, paste the plain text content in the center, and close the tag so the computer knows you're done using it.

HTML stands for HyperText Markup Language the "Markup Language" means using a programming language to perform a function, HTML uses tags to identify different types of content and the purpose each serves for a website. All web pages consist of a series of HTML tags that identify each type of content on the page. Each content type on the page is "wrapped" in HTML tags.

Once a tag is opened, all subsequent content is considered part of that tag until the tag is "closed". Add the paragraph closing tag when the paragraph ends. Note that closing tags look the same as opening tags, except that there is a slash after the left angle bracket. Here is an example you can use HTML to add headings, format paragraphs, control line breaks, create lists, highlight text, create special characters, insert images, create links, create tables, control styles, and more can do.

To learn something more about coding in HTML, we recommend reading the basic HTML guide and taking advantage of Udemy, Pluralsight, Codeacdemy's free courses, and other resources, but let's move on to CSS for now. This programming language determines how HTML elements of the website are actually displayed on the front end of the page.

CSS

HTML provides the raw tools you need to structure your website's content. CSS, on the other hand, helps us style our content so that it appears to the user as intended. These languages are always kept separate so that the website is built correctly before being reformatted. Again, check out free courses and resources to learn more about coding in CSS. But let's talk a little bit about JavaScript here.

Stylesheet

A stylesheet is a set of some CSS rules used to control the layout of a web page or document. Internal stylesheets are placed inside a <style> element inside the <head> of a web page document, the external stylesheets are placed inside a separate .css file, which is applied to a document by referencing the file inside a <link> element in the document head. External stylesheets are preferred because they allow to control the styling of multiple pages from one place, than having to repeat the CSS across each page.

Adding Styles Using CSS

It is the styling information can either be attached as a separate document or embedded in the document itself. These are the three methods of implementing styling in an HTML document:

- Inline styles – It is used in the style attribute in the HTML start tag.

- Embedded style – It is used in the <style> element in the head section of the document.

- External stylesheet – It is used in the <link> element, pointing to an external CSS file.

Inline Styles

Inline styles are used to apply unique style rules to an element by inserting CSS rules directly into the start tag.[9] It can attach to an element using the style attribute.

The style attribute contains a number of CSS property-value pairs. Each property: value pair is separated by a semicolon (;), just as you would write in an inline or external style list. But everything must be on one line, i.e. without a line break after a semicolon.

```
<!DOCTYPE HTML>
<html>
  <head>
    <meta  content="text/HTML; HTTP-equiv="Content-
Type"  charset=utf-8">
    <title>Title of the document</title>
    <style>
    body{
      width:500px;
      margin:0 auto,
    }
    </style>
  </head>

  <body>
    <h1> Nesting HTML Elements </h1>
    <h1 style="color:red; font-size:20px;">This is a
heading in red color with 30 font size</h1>
    <p style="color:green; font-size:28px;">This is a
paragraph in green with 18 font size </p>
    <div style="color:yellow; font-size:28px;">This is
div the text in the div will be of yellow with 28 font
</div>

</html>
```

Embedded Stylesheets
Embedded are also called as internal stylesheets that only affect the document they are embedded into. Embedded stylesheets are defined in the <head> tag of the document using the <style> tag. You can define various number of <style> elements in the <head> section.

```
<!DOCTYPE HTML>
<html>
  <head>
    <meta content="text/HTML;  HTTP-equiv="Content-
Type" charset=utf-8">
```

```
<title>Title of the document</title>
<style>
body{
   width:500px;
   margin:0 auto;
   background-color: YellowGreen;
}
h1 { color: blue; }
    p { color: red; }

</style>
</head>

<body>
  <h1> HTML Elements </h1>
  <h1 >This is a heading in red color with 30 font
size</h1>
  <p >This is a paragraph in green with 18 font size
</p>
  <div>This is div the text in the div will be of
yellow with 28 font </div>

</html>
```

External Styles

An external stylesheet is used when the style is applied to many pages. An external stylesheet contains all of the style rules in a separate document that you can link to from any HTML document on your website. External stylesheets are the most flexible because with an external stylesheet you can change the look of your entire site by updating just one file. You can connect external stylesheets in two ways such as linking and importing.

Index.html

```
<!DOCTYPE HTML>
<html>
  <head>
    <meta content="text/HTML; HTTP-equiv="Content-
Type"; charset=utf-8">
    <title>Title of the document</title>
 <link href="style.css" rel="stylesheet">

  </head>
```

```
<body>
    <h1> Nesting HTML Elements </h1>
    <h1 >This is a heading in red color with 30 font
size</h1>
    <p >This is a paragraph in green with 18 font size
</p>
    <div>This is div the text in the div will be of
yellow with 28 font </div>

</html>
```

Style.css

```
<style>
  body{
    width:500px;
    margin:0 auto;
    background-color: YellowGreen;
  }
  h1 { color: blue; }
      p { color: red; }

  </style>
```

Importing External Stylesheets

The @import rule is another way to load an external stylesheet.[10] The @import directive instructs the browser to load an external stylesheet and apply its styles.

You can use it in two ways. The easiest method is to use it in the <style> element in the <head> section. Note that additional CSS rules can still be included in the <style> element.

First example:

```
<style>
    @import URL("css/style.css");
    p {
        color: blue;
        font-size: 16px;
    }
</style>
```

Second example:

```
@import URL("css/layout.css");
@import URL("css/color.css");
body {
    color: blue;
    font-size: 14px;
}
```

CSS COMMENTS

CSS comments are not visible in the browser but may be helpful in writing your source code.[11] Comments are also used to explain the code and can be helpful if you edit the source code later. Comments ignored by browsers. CSS comments are embedded within the <style> element, and begin with / / and end with * /:

Example:

```
/* This is a one-line comment */
p {
  color: red;
}
```

You can add comments where you want to code.

Example:

```
p {

    color: red;    /* * Set text color in red  */
}

/* This
many lines
comment

*/

p {
  color: red;
}
```

CSS SELECTORS

CSS selector is for matching features on a web page.[12] The style rules connected with that selector will apply to items such as the pattern. Choices are one of the most important CSS features as they allow you to direct certain elements to your web page in a variety of ways to style them.

A few types of selectors are available in CSS, let's take a closer look.

Universal Selector

It is indicated by a star (*) that corresponds to each part of the page. The universal selector may be removed if other conditions are present in the feature. This filter is often used to remove automatic genes and pads from elements for quick testing.

Let's try the following example to understand how it basically works.

```
*  {
    margin: 0;
    padding: 0;
}
```

The style rules within the selector * will apply to everything in the document.

Element Type Selectors

It is the same as every element in a document and the name of the corresponding element type. Let's try an example to see how it really works.

```
p {
    color: blue;
}
```

ID Selector

The ID selector is used to describe style rules for one or more items. The ID selector is defined by a hash (#) symbol that is immediately followed by the ID value.

Example:

```
#text{
    color: red;
}
```

This style rule gives the text the object in red, its ID identifier being set as default.

Class Selectors

It is used to select any HTML component with a class attribute. All features with that class will be formatted according to a defined rule. The class selector is defined by an intermediate symbol (.). That is immediately followed by a class value.

Example:

```
.green {
    color: blue;
}
```

Descendant Selectors

You can use these options if you need to select an interest-bearing element of another element, for example, if you want to define only those anchors contained in the random list, rather than directing all anchor elements. Let's try an example to see how it works.

```
ul.menu li a {
    text-decoration: none;
}
h1 em {
    color: green;
}
```

The style rules within the selector ul.menu li a apply only to those elements <a> contained within the <ul> element that has a class .menu, and that does not affect other links within the document. Similarly, style rules within the h1 em selector will only apply to those elements of <em> content contained within the element of <h1> and which do not affect other elements of <em>.

Child Selectors

The child selector is used to select only those specific child items for a particular feature. The children's selector is made up of two or more selectors that are separated by a larger symbol (>). You can use this selector, for example, to select the first level of list items within a nested list with more than one level. Let's look at an example to see how it works.

```
ul > li {
    list-style: circle;
}
ul > li ol {
    list-style: none;
}
```

The style rule inside the selector, such as ul > li applied to only those <li> elements that direct children of the <ul> elements, has no effect on other list elements.

Adjacent Sibling Selectors

Adjacent sibling selectors are used to select its sibling elements (i.e. elements at the same level). This selector has a syntax such as: E1 + E2, where E2 is the target selector.

The h1 + p selector in the following example will select <p> elements only if the <h1> and <p> elements can share the same parent in the document tree and <h1> precedes the <p> section immediately. This means that only those sections that come immediately after each <h1> title will have corresponding style rules. Let's see how this option really works.

Example:

```
h1 + p {
    color: blue;
    font-size: 18px;
}
ul.text + p {
    color: black;
    font-size: 30px;
}
```

Standard Sibling Selectors

The standard sibling selector is similar to the nearest sibling selector (E1 + E2), but less powerful. The standard sibling selector is made up of two simple picks separated by a tilde (~) character. It can be written as follows: E1 ~ E2, where E2 is the purpose of the selector.

The h1 ~ p selector in the example below will select all the <p> features preceded by the <h1> section, where all the features share the same parent in the document tree.

```
h1 ~ p {
    color: blue;
    font-size: 18px;
}
ul.task ~ p {
    color: #f0f;
    text-indent: 30px;
}
```

Grouping Selectors

Usually, a few selectors on a stylesheet share declarations of the same style rules. You can group them with a comma-separated list to narrow the code to your stylesheet. It also prevents other users from repeating the same style rules over and over again.

Let's take a look:

```
h1 {
    font-size: 36px;
    font-weight: normal;
}
h2 {
    font-size: 28px;
    font-weight: normal;
}
h3 {
    font-size: 22px;
    font-weight: normal;
}
```

JAVASCRIPT

JavaScript is a more complex language than HTML and CSS and was released in beta only in 1995.[13] JavaScript is now used by almost every website on the web, as it is supported by all modern web browsers and has more powerful and complex capabilities.

It is a logic-based programming language that can be used to modify the content of websites to behave differently depending on user actions.

Common uses of JavaScript include confirmation boxes, calls to action, and adding new identities to existing information.

Adding JavaScript to HTML Documents

You can include JavaScript code in your HTML documents using a special HTML or section of the HTML, depending on when the JavaScript should be loaded.[14] JavaScript code can generally be placed in the section of the document and excluded from the body of the HTML document.

However, if the script needs to run at a specific point in the layout of the page (such as when generating content using document.write), where you want the script to be called (usually in the section) should be placed as given below.

```
<!DOCTYPE html>
<html lang="en-US">

<head>
    <meta charset="UTF-8">
    <meta name="viewport" content="width=device-width,
initial-scale=1">
    <title> JavaScript in HTML </title>
</head>

<body>

</body>
 <script>
    let d = new Date();
alert("Today's date is " + d);
</script>
</html>
```

> **127.0.0.1:5500 says**
>
> Today's date is Tue Sep 06 2022 10:24:07 GMT+0530 (India Standard Time)
>
> OK

JavaScript in HTML.

The above example pops up the alert dialog box when it loads. You can press ok button to stop loading page.

```
<!DOCTYPE html>
<html lang="en-US">

<head>
    <meta charset="UTF-8">
    <meta name="viewport" content="width=device-width,
initial-scale=1">
    <title> JavaScript in HTML </title>
</head>

<body>
    <h2> Date is showing using document.body.
innerHTML</h2>
</body>
 <script>
    let d = new Date();
    document.body.innerHTML = "<h3>Today's date is
" + d + "</h3>"
</script>
</html>
```

The output for the above would look similar to the following.

Today's date is Mon Sep 19 2022 17:07:36 GMT+0530 (India Standard Time)

Date time.

Another example:

```
<!DOCTYPE html>
<html lang="en-US">

<head>
    <meta charset="UTF-8">
    <meta name="viewport" content="width=device-
width, initial-scale=1">
    <title> JavaScript in HTML </title>
</head>
```

```
<body>
    <h2> Date is showing using document
.getElementById.innerHTML</h2>
  <div id="show-date"></div>
</body>
 <script>
    let d = new Date();
    document.getElementById('show-date').innerHTML
= "<h4>Today's date is " + d + "</h4>"
</script>
</html>
```

The output for the above would look similar to the following.

Date is showing using document.getElementById.innerHTML

Today's date is Mon Sep 19 2022 17:05:02 GMT+0530 (India Standard Time)

Date time.

Small scripts or scripts that only run on one page work well in HTML files, but for large scripts or scripts that are used on many pages, this can be hard to read when pasting, so not much but also it is not an effective solution. The next we will describe how to handle different JavaScript files within the HTML document.

Let's know how to connect a JavaScript document to an HTML document, by creating a small web page. It consists of script.js in the js/ directory, style.css in the css/ directory, and the main file index.html in the root of the project. The folder structure will look like this given below.

```
project/
├── css/
│   └── style.css
├── js/
│   └── script.js
└── index.html
```

In the above section, we have already discussed how to add .js and .css files in HTML document. JavaScript may be a client-side scripting language, suggesting that the client's browser handles processing ASCII text files rather than online servers. With the help of JavaScript, websites can be loaded without connecting to the primary server.

The pros of JavaScript are:[15]

- JavaScript is easy to understand. Both users and developers will find the structure simple. Moreover, it is very easy to implement and saves web developers a lot of money when creating dynamic content.

- It integrates seamlessly with other programming languages; many developers prefer it to create a wide variety of applications.

- It is an "interpreted" language, reducing the time it takes to compile in other programming languages such as Java.

The cons of JavaScript are:

- Although some editors allow for debugging, they are not as effective as editors for C or C++.

- It does not support multiple inheritances; only one inheritance is supported.

- The code needs to run on various platforms before publication.

Now let's move deeper into the DOM in HTML for making your JavaScript more clean and effective.

DOM

he Document Object Model (DOM) is a data representation of the objects that make up the structure and content of documents on the Web.[16] This guide introduces the DOM, how it represents an in-memory HTML document. The DOM is a programming interface for Web documents. It can render the page so that the program can change the structure, style, and content of the document. DOM represents documents as nodes and objects. It allows programming languages to interact with the page.

All properties, methods, and events that can be used to edit and create web pages are grouped into objects. For example, the DOM that represents the document itself, all table objects that implement the HTML Table Element DOM interface for accessing HTML tables, etc. are objects.

The DOM is using multiple APIs that work together. The Core DOM defines entities that describe each document and the objects it contains. It will be extended by other APIs as needed to add new features and functionality to the DOM. For example, the DOM API adds support for rendering HTML documents to the core DOM, and the SVG API adds support for rendering SVG documents.

It is not a programming language, but without the DOM the JavaScript language would have no model or concept of web pages, HTML documents, SVG documents, and their parts. The entire document, headers, tables within the document, table headings, text within table cells, and all other elements within the document are part of the DOM for that document. They can be accessed and manipulated using the DOM and scripting languages such as JavaScript.

ACCESS TO DOM

You do not need to have anything special to start using DOM. You can use the API directly in JavaScript from what's called a script, which is a program run by the browser. When you create a script, either embedded in a <script> element or included in a web page, you can immediately start using the document API or window objects to manipulate the document itself or any of the various elements on the web page (the following document elements). Your DOM programming can be something as simple as the following example, which displays a message to the console log using the console.log() function.

BASIC DATA TYPES

This page attempts to explain various objects and types in simple terms. However, you must be aware of the different types of data passed through the API. The following table describes these data types.

- Data Types (Interfaces)
- Documents
- Nodes
- Elements
- Node Lists
- Attributes
- NamedNodeMap

DOM INTERFACES

It describes the objects and realities you can use to manipulate the DOM hierarchy.[17] There are various points where understanding how these work can be confusing. For example, an object representing an HTML form element gets its name property from the HTMLFormElement interface but gets its className property from the HTMLElement interface. In either case, the required properties are on that form object.

However, the relationship between objects and the interfaces they implement in the DOM can be confusing, so this section attempts to describe the actual interfaces in the DOM specification and how they are exposed.

CORE INTERFACES

Here is the list of the commonly used interfaces in the DOM. The Document and Window objects are the objects with the commonly used interfaces in DOM programming. Simply put, the window object represents something like a browser; the document object is the root of the document itself. Element inherits from the general Node interfaces and combines these two interfaces to provide many methods and properties for use on individual elements.

The following is a full list of common APIs using the DOM:

- document.querySelector(selector)
- document.querySelectorAll(name)
- document.createElement(name)
- parentNode.appendChild(node)
- element.innerHTML
- element.style.left
- element.setAttribute()
- element.getAttribute()
- element.addEventListener()
- window.content
- Window.onload
- window.scrollTo()

CHAPTER SUMMARY

In this chapter, we discussed various topics related to HTML such as web scripting, the difference between scripting and programming, dynamic elements, relation between css and js, comments, various selectors, and JavaScript.

NOTES

1. Web Scripting – https://www.informit.com/articles/article.aspx?p=2952622, accessed on September 5, 2022.
2. Scripts – https://www.informit.com/articles/article.aspx?p=2952622, accessed on September 5, 2022.
3. Scripts – https://qatestlab.com/resources/knowledge-center/scripting-languages-aim/, accessed on September 5, 2022.
4. Web Scripting and its types – https://www.geeksforgeeks.org/web-scripting-and-its-types/, accessed on September 5, 2022.
5. Dynamic HTML – https://www.techtarget.com/whatis/definition/dynamic-HTML, accessed on September 5, 2022.
6. Correlation with CSS, JavaScript – https://www.freecodecamp.org/news/the-relationship-between-html-css-and-javascript-explained-by-building-a-city-a73a69c6343/, accessed on September 5, 2022.
7. HTML – https://blog.hubspot.com/marketing/web-design-html-css-javascript, accessed on September 5, 2022.
8. HTML Works – https://www.byjusfutureschool.com/blog/what-is-html-what-are-the-benefits-uses-features-of-html-in-real-world/, accessed on September 5, 2022.
9. Inline Style – https://www.w3schools.com/html/html_css.asp, accessed on September 5, 2022.
10. CSS Media – https://www.tutorialspoint.com/importing-external-style-sheets-in-css, accessed on September 5, 2022.
11. CSS Comments – https://www.w3schools.com/css/css_comments.asp, accessed on September 6, 2022.
12. CSS Selector – https://developer.mozilla.org/en-US/docs/Learn/CSS/Building_blocks/Selectors/Type_Class_and_ID_Selectors, accessed on September 6, 2022.
13. JavaScript – https://blog.hubspot.com/marketing/web-design-html-css-javascript, accessed on September 5, 2022.
14. Adding JavaScript – https://www.digitalocean.com/community/tutorials/how-to-add-javascript-to-html, accessed on September 6, 2022.
15. Pros and Cons – https://www.tutorialspoint.com/advantages-and-disadvantages-of-javascript, accessed on September 6, 2022.
16. HTML DOM – https://developer.mozilla.org/en-US/docs/Web/API/Document_Object_Model/Introduction, accessed on September 6, 2022.
17. DOM – https://developer.mozilla.org/en-US/docs/Web/API/Document_Object_Model/Introduction, accessed on September 6, 2022.

Code Optimization

IN THIS CHAPTER

➤ Introduction

➤ Writing HTML in Code

➤ Security and Hardening Ideas

In the previous chapter, we have shared the relationship between the HTML with CSS and JS. This chapter provides useful techniques for improving frontend optimization. By focusing on well clean code, compressing images, minimizing external requests, implementing a CDN, and a few other methods, you can also improve your website's speed and overall performance increase.

INTRODUCTION

Every day, millions of websites are visited for various reasons. Unfortunately, many of these websites are difficult to use with poorly optimized websites suffering from slow loading times, not mobile friendly and browser incompatibilities.

The frontend is the first place you meet your users. However, if your website takes too long to load, don't wait. No one visits and rates your slow websites. The page feel and overall performance of your website, such as page speed, are important ranking factors for search engines. Better performance means a better chance for your audience to find you. Optimizing your website related to speed is very important to improve the customer

DOI: 10.1201/9781003357537-3

experience. Now we're sharing how we actually improved the performance of our own websites.

Clean Up the HTML Document

HTML is the backbone of almost every website.[1] It allows you to format web pages using headings, subheadings, lists, and other useful features for organizing text. You can also create various attractive graphics with the latest HTML5 updates.

HTML is easy for web crawlers (Google bot, Bing bot, Slurp bot) to read, so search engines can be updated with your site's content in a timely manner. When working with HTML, you should try to write in a way that is concise and effective. Extra, when it comes to referencing other resources in an HTML document, there are some best practices you should follow.

Combining Files

You can commonly combine used CSS scripts into one file so that you only had to reference one file instead of multiple files in your HTML.

Correct CSS Placement

Web designers tend to create CSS Stylesheet after the main HTML skeleton of a web page has been created.[2] As a result, CSS components can be placed at the bottom of the document. However, it is recommended to place the CSS at the beginning of the header of the HTML document to ensure progressive rendering.

```
<head>
    <link href='https://your_website.com/css/style.
css' rel='stylesheet' type='text/css'>
</head>
```

Best practice with CSS and JavaScript is to avoid inlining code. When you embed the code, you put the CSS in the style tag and use the JavaScript in the script tags. It increases the amount of code that must be loaded every time your website is updated.

Correcting JavaScript Placement

Conversely, placing JavaScript attributes at the top of the head tag or HTML document blocks HTML and CSS elements from loading. This error can cause visitors to wait on a blank page and leave your site in a hurry. You can work around related to this issue by placing the JavaScript attribute at the end of your HTML code. It is used with CSS and JavaScript attributes that can slow down the website. CSS and JavaScript attributes can change website for the better, but you should pay special attention and use them correctly.

Limiting External HTTP Requests

The majority of web page load time comes from external HTTP requests.[3] The loading speed of external resources may vary depending on the hosting provider's server infrastructure, location, etc. To reducing external HTTP requests is to explore site with a minimal view. You can go through all functions of the website and remove any features that don't improve your visitor's experience. You should various avoid these things in your code such as:

- Unnecessary images

- Unnecessary JavaScript

- Excessive CSS

- Unnecessary plugins

CDN Factor

CDNs can also improve server response times by pre-pooling connections and keeping them open across sessions. A CDN by itself does not reduce the number of requests, but pre-pooling improves performance by eliminating the latency associated with closing and reopening TCP connections.

File Compression

Every page on a website consists of a collection of HTML, JavaScript, CSS, and (possibly) other code files.[4] The large complex the page, the larger the code file and the longer it takes to load.

File compression can reduce these files to a fraction of their original size, making your website more responsive. Preferred for its fast encode/decode times and high compression ratio, gzip is the most popular choice for file compression. Code files can be reduced by up to 60% or 80%.

Code Minification

Minification is a process that recognizes the difference between how developers write code and how machines read it. It is easy for reading, with spaces, line breaks, and comments – machines can read it without any of these elements, making them nonessential characters.

Image Enhancement

Caching and compression are the two common image enhancement methods, with caching being the more efficient of the two.[5] This is because, unlike code files, all image formats are already compressed.

Therefore, to further reduce the file size of an image, the data in that image must be modified by removing some header information or reducing the quality of the original image. This is called lossy compression.

Division into Small Components

Now our frontend can split into many components.[6] These small components are the part of the page that has a specific functionality: image gallery view, main menu view, main content view, and so on. Each component can be simple (just a static template) or more complex, with interactions and JavaScript, reacting to clicks, managing the state of the element (shown or hidden), loading and preparing a new element (new image or gallery image).

Analysis of the Frontend Code

The thing need to do is to understand how the frontend code is built. The technical pattern of the guide was as follows:

- All frontend components were compiled as one application (or one big JS file).

- All CSS was compiled as one big CSS file.

- This pattern was previously used everywhere and is optimized for HTTP1.

HTTP1 recommendations suggest minimizing the number of requests to the server and loading a few large files instead of a few small files. Because creating a new request (connecting to the server) can be time-consuming (regardless of file size) and many simultaneous requests are not allowed. This is why so many web designs encapsulate their JavaScript and CSS in a single file.

HTTP2 to Help Frontend Developers

Modern servers today provide a new version of the HTTP protocol (HTTP2), and web browsers increasingly take advantage of the multithreaded and multicore capabilities of modern computers and mobile devices.[7] This means we can process even more data at the same time.

The HTTP2 protocol has been greatly improved.

- The protocol can accept multiple simultaneous requests by reusing the actual connection.

- No need to negotiate and re-establish the connection on every request. Lost time disappears.

- Many files (from many requests) can be sent in one response (multiplexing) also provides better compression (30% improvement).

Enable Preloading

Prefetching can improve visitors' browsing experience by loading necessary resources and related data before they are needed. There are three main types of preloading:

- Prefetching the link

- DNS prefetching

- Pre-rendering

With prefetching, URLs, CSS, images, and JavaScript are collected for each link before you even leave the current web page. This ensures that visitors can use the links to navigate between pages with minimal loading time.

Fortunately, enabling prefetching is easy. Depending on the type of prefetching you want to enable, you can add the rel="prefetch", rel="dns-prefetch", or rel="prerender" tag to the link attributes in your site's HTML code.

PRELOAD AND PREFETCH IN HTML

Loading materials on a page is an important part of achieving optimal website performance and a smooth user experience. Real-world applications typically load multiple CSS files, fonts, JavaScript, and images. These resources block rendering by default, which degrades loading performance.

You will get to explore a new feature called resource tips such as prefetch. These resource tips will help you overcome render blocking.

Understanding Renders Blocking

When a resource request blocks rendering, it means that the window. onload event will not fire until that request has finished.[8] In modern single-page applications, most assets such as CSS and JavaScript files along with images rely on this event to start working. This means that parts of the user interface will not start to render or appear on the screen until the render-blocking requests have finished loading.

To see this in action, we create an HTML file with standard HTML. This can be done in code editor of choice as shown in the following example:

```
<!DOCTYPE html>
<html lang="en-US">

<head>
    <meta charset="UTF-8">
    <meta content="width=device-width, initial-
scale=1" name="viewport"
    <title> JavaScript in HTML </title>>
    <link rel="stylesheet" href='https://fonts.
googleapis.com/css?family=Roboto:400,600|Material&+
Icons'>
    <style>
      html {
        font-family: Roboto;
      }
    </style>
</head>

<body>
<p> You are leaning Preload and Prefetch in HTML </p>

<script>
  window.onload = function () {
    console.log('Your page is fully loaded');
  }
</script>
</body>
</html>
```

To see render blocking in action, add <script> tags to the <body>. Create a JavaScript function using window.onload that will give console. log message: "Your page is fully loaded" as given above in the code.

After the code is installed, open the HTML file in Chrome. Next, open Developer Tools and go to the Network tab. Your loaded message is logged to the console immediately after the CSS file is loaded, as shown in the following image given below.

You are leaning Preload and Prefetch in HTML.

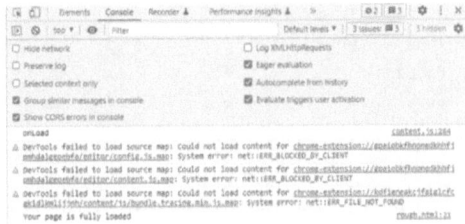

Preload and prefetch in HTML.

Preload Resources

To avoid default rendering blocking and to ensure that page resources such as fonts and CSS start loading early in the page's lifecycle, you'll need to implement preloading. The attribute rel="preload" value is used to preload assets. It can be used on several file formats, including CSS, JS, fonts, images, and more. It is depending on the type of file you want to preload, you may also need to include the appropriate as attribute along with rel="preload". For the CSS, as = will need to be set to "style". In the case of JavaScript, as= will need to be set to "script". Go back to the HTML file and change the previous <link>. Set rel equal to "bias". Add as an attribute set equal to "style".

```
<link rel="preload" "href='https://fonts.googleapis.
com/css?family=Roboto:400,600|Material&+Icons'
as="style" onload="this.rel = 'stylesheet' >
```

Setting the rel attribute to the stylesheet on load tells the browser to use the resource. Since it has already been downloaded to memory, it does not download again. Since the onload relies on JavaScript, add <noscript> tags that contain the original <link> tags with rel set to "stylesheet".

```
<link
 rel="
style
sheet"
 rel="preload"
    href='https://fonts.googleapis.com/css?family=Robo
to:400,600|Material&+Icons'
```

```
  as="style"
  onload="this.rel = 'stylesheet
 ' "
 >
<noscript>
  <link
    >
</noscript>
```

This ensures that the font is displayed if JavaScript is disabled or fails to load. Now you know how to prefetch website assets. There are times when you'll want to preload resources instead.

CSS preloading and loading can help improve website performance. You can also apply preloading to your JavaScript. Preloading JavaScript is different from preloading CSS resources.

Preload JavaScript

Prefetching JavaScript resources is done differently. An example, taken from the Google Developers on preloading, is given below.

```
<link rel="preload" href="user_later.js"
as="script">
<!-- ... -->
<script>
  var usedLaterScript = document.
createElement('script');
  usedLaterScript.src = 'used-later.js';
  document.body.appendChild(usedLaterScript);
</script>
```

The important step is to set the file's src attribute and insert it into the DOM.

Compress Files (gzip Compression)

While many CDN services compress your files for you, if you're not using a CDN, consider using a file compression method on origin server to improve frontend optimization. File compression ensures that your website content is lightweight and easy to work with. One of the most used file compression ways is gzip. This is a good method for reducing the size of documents, audio files, PNG images, and other large files that have not yet been compressed.

Brotli is file compression algorithm that is new but growing in popularity. The open-source algorithm is updated by software engineers from Google and other organizations. It has proven to compress files at a much better ratio than other existing methods.

Highlight of Brotli
Compression has come in a long way in the past few years and Brotli is now at the forefront of this category. Here are a few strengths that make Brotli a leader in compression:

- Brotli is independent of CPU type, operating system, file system, and character set and can produce a compression ratio is comparable to the good compression methods available, and most importantly, it is significantly better than gzip.

- It decompresses much faster than the current LZMA implementation.

The results of Google's compression algorithm study shows that Brotli achieved the best results in compression ratio, compression speed, and decompression speed.

Optimize Your Images
For people who aren't used to frontend optimization methods, images can be a website killer. Massive photo albums and large high-resolution images on website can disrupt the rendering process. High-resolution images that are not optimized can weigh several megabytes. So, proper optimization will allow you to improve the frontend performance of your website.

Each image file contains a wealth of information unrelated to the actual photo or image. For JPEG photos, the file contains data, location, camera specifications, and other trivial information. You can streamline the lengthy image-loading process by removing this redundant image data using optimization tools like Optimus. Optimus uses intelligent compression in that it uses lossless optimization of PNG images.

LOSSY VS. LOSSLESS COMPRESSION

When it comes to reducing the size of images for the web, there are different types of compression to choose from. Here, we will look at lossy vs. lossless compression and the pros and cons of both the methods.

Lossy Compression

Lossy compression refers to compression where some data from the original file (JPEG) is lost. This process is irreversible, once you convert to a loss you cannot go back. And the more compress it, the more it degrades. JPEG and GIF are lossy image formats. By default, WordPress uses 90% lossy compression to optimize JPEG images when creating preview images. One of the biggest obvious benefits of using lossy compression is that it results in a significantly reduced file size (smaller than a lossless compression method), but it also means a loss of quality.

Lossless Compression

Lossless compression helps to reduce the file size without losing quality. This method of reducing file sizes can be applied to both image and audio files. While JPEG and MP3 use lossy compression, newer compression algorithms such as JPEG 2000 and Apple Lossless compression can use to create lossless compressed files.

Lossless compression essentially overwrites the original file data more efficiently. However, because there is no quality loss, the resulting files are usually much larger than lossy image and audio files. For example, a file compressed using compression may be one-tenth the size of the original, while lossless compression is to produce a file smaller than half the original size.

Use a Minimalist Framework

Unless you're building your website with only your own coding knowledge, you can avoid many amateur frontend optimization mistakes by using a good frontend interface. Although some of the larger and better-known frameworks come with a number of additional features and options, web project may not require them all.

That's why it's good to determine what features in your project require and start with a framework that can provide features while remaining lightweight. Some of the most recently designed frameworks used to concise HTML, CSS, and JavaScript.

Here are some examples of minimalistic frameworks that provide fast loading:

- Pure
- Foundation

- Skeleton

- Milligram

Create Picture Sprites

Icons, button backgrounds, checkmarks, and arrows all take up little space but require a lot of server requests. To give each icon separately, paste them into sprites and reload them at once.

Apply Lazy Load

The term lazy loading applies to both scripts and styles, but images are often referred to.[9] The fad of huge landing pages with a dozen screens and megabytes of images is not working. Loading tons of data is a problem; it doesn't matter how fast Internet we have. The idea behind lazy loading is to load resources only when you actually need them. In the case of images, those images that are currently visible are loaded.

Insert JavaScript at the Bottom of the Page

The browser must download the content before the JS. If you have one Single Page Application, then there will be no profit from this advice.

Include Styles Dynamically

HTML can be so scary that without styles it will take users a quarter of a second to escape the site.

Use CSS Animations Instead of JavaScript

Sometimes it's very cool to create a tricky animation in JS. CSS3 has long been held in huge esteem, feel free to use transitions and keyframes. Of course, you should consider the support of these features by the required browsers. Animations are often decorative and supplementary. If the use of browser doesn't support CSS transitions, they will be shown a static image. However, if the implementation of the animation is necessary, then it is worth duplicating it using JavaScript.

Minify CSS, JavaScript, and HTML

Minification techniques can help you remove unnecessary characters in a file. When you write code in the editor, you probably use indentation and notes. These methods keep the code clean and readable, but they also add extra bytes to the document. CSS, JS, and HTML minification involves removing all unnecessary characters from a file, which will help reduce its size and thereby speed up loading. Examples of what is removed during file minification include:

- Blank characters

- Comments

- End of lines

- Block separators

WRITING HTML IN CODE

Declare DOCTYPE

Declaring a DOCTYPE used to be a tough process. However, HTML5 made things much simpler. Now, just add the following line to the top of your web page to let browsers know that it should be interpreted as HTML5.

```
<!DOCTYPE html>
```

In some old websites that have not been updated for a while may still use older standards to declare the DOCTYPE. Using the line above is the correct way to do it in HTML5. Just remember that it must come before everything, even before the <html> tag.

Example:

```
<!DOCTYPE html>
<html lang="en">
<head>
  <meta charset="UTF-8">
  <meta http-equiv="X-UA-Compatible"
content="IE=edge">
  <meta content="width=device-width, initial-
scale=1.0" name="viewport" >
  <title>Document</title>
</head>
<body>
  <!--content -->
</body>
</html>
```

The doctype declaration should be the thing in your HTML documents. The doctype declaration informs the browser about the XHTML standards you will be using and helps it correctly read and render your markup. You can also write your doctype like this.

```
<!DOCTYPE html PUBLIC "-//W3C//DTD XHTML 1.0 Strict//
EN", "http://www.w3.org/TR/xhtml1/DTD/xhtml1-strict.
dtd">
```

Use Meaningful Title Tags and Other Tags

The <title> tag helps to make a web page more meaningful and search engine friendly. For example, the content inside the <title> tag will appear on the Google search engine results page as well as in the web browser bar and tabs.

```
<title> Best HTML Coding Practices </title>
```

This will display on the Google browser when your search is related to this. Every part of your website should be created using the HTML5 markup that is most appropriate for the content. It's best to avoid overusing generic tags like <div> when a more descriptive tag like <section>, <article>, and so on could exist for the task.

Use the Right Document Structure

HTML documents will still work without elements such as <html>, <head>, and <body>.[10] However, pages do not display correctly in all browsers, so it is important that you use the correct document structure.

If you've been using HTML for a while, you know that every piece of HTML must be wrapped in HTML tags. The opening <html> tag should appear first and the closing </html> tag should appear at the bottom of the document. Every other piece of HTML should appear between these two tags.

```
<!DOCTYPE html>
<html lang="en">
<head>
  <meta charset="UTF-8">
  <meta http-equiv="X-UA-Compatible"
content="IE=edge">
```

```
  <meta  content="width=device-width, initial-
scale=1.0" name="viewport">
  <title>Document</title>
</head>
<body>
  <!—content -->
</body>
</html>
```

The head element is the first element that appears after the opening HTML tag. We put all things like the page title and metadata in the document head, add JavaScript to our page using the script tag, and [link] to external stylesheets (CSS, CDN links) and other resources.

On most web pages, the head element is a very busy place. That's why we've created a tutorial that explains the tags that typically appear in the head element and what those tags are used for.

All content that is visible on a web page is nestled between the opening and closing body tags. The body is the primary container of content that makes up a web page.

Until HTML5, that was pretty much it for the basic structure of an HTML document. All of our code was wrapped between body tags and styled with CSS. Now that HTML5 has widespread support among modern browsers, it's time to implement new HTML5 tags that will give HTML documents a much more meaningful structure.

```
<!DOCTYPE html>
<html lang="en">
<head>
  <meta charset="UTF-8">
  <meta http-equiv="X-UA-Compatible"
content="IE=edge">
  <meta content="width=device-width, initial-
scale=1.0" name="viewport" >
  <title> The title of the document</title>
  <link href="style.css" rel="stylesheet">
</head>
<body>
  <!—content -->
  <script src="script.js" rel="text/javascript">
</script>
</body>
</html>
```

To define the structure and content of a web page. The elements we are going to cover include:

- header
- main
- nav
- article
- section
- aside
- address
- footer

Using these elements is not as complicated as it might seem at first view. We will quickly walk through each new element and then create an HTML template that you can use these new tags to add rich semantic meaning to your markup.

HTML Structure

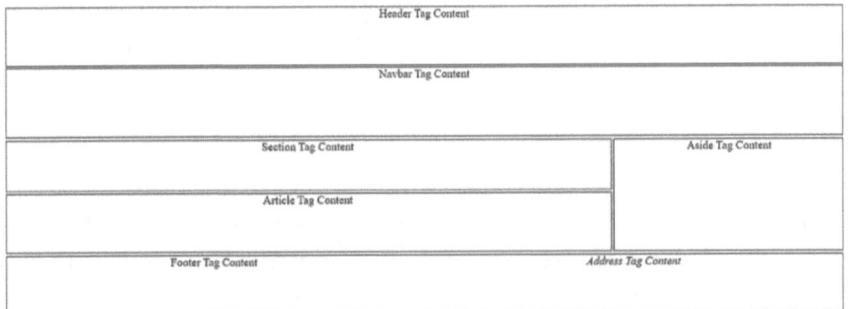

HTML full structure.

<header>

The header element is used to contain the content that appears at the top of each page of your website: a logo, tagline, call to action, and possibly a navigation menu. In most cases, the header element is best placed as a direct child of the body element, but it's also fine to place it inside the main element if you want.

<main>

Use the main element between the header and footer elements to contain the primary content of your web page. The main element cannot be a child of an article, side element, header, footer, or navigation element. Instead, it can be a direct descendant of the body element.

It's also okay to use more than one main element on a web page for making more partitions. For example, if your index page contains your five most recent posts, it would be a better idea to wrap each post in its own main element.

<nav>

Navigation menus are commonly located at the top of a web page, in a sidebar, or in the footer of a page. Wherever you place your navigation menu, wrap it in navigation tags. Note that you don't need to use navigation tags for every link, only for blocks of links that allow site-wide navigation or site-specific navigation.

<article>

If your page contains blog, articles, or any other content that could just as well appear on another site as content, wrap that content in an article. You can use an article element almost anywhere other than nestled within an address element, but an article element will be a direct child of a parent element or a section element that is a direct child of a parent element.

<section>

The section element is used to identify the content that is a major subsection of a larger entity. For example, if you have a site that contains various text in HTML format, it would make sense to wrap each in a section element. Similarly, if you have a sidebar that contains four sections then it would be fine to wrap each of those four sections in section tags because written the sidebar content outline would include a line item for each of the four sections.

There might be some confusion about when to use a section and when to use a div. Here are some rules:

- The div element has no special meaning. It is often used as a block of children's elements.

- Introduced in the HTML5 standard, the section element is used to group together related elements, such as a subsection of a long article.

- In short, the section element provides a more semantic syntax than the div element.

<aside>

If your website contains information that is not directly related to the main content of the page, it would be a good idea to wrap this information in tags such as aside tags.

<address>

The address tag gives contact information for the nearest parent article or body element that contains it. You can use the address element inside the article to enter contact information for the author of the article. Use it outside of the article in main or footer elements, or as a direct child of the body element also provide contact information for the site owner.

<footer>

The footer appears at the last of a section of a document. The footer tag is a direct descendant of the body tag, but it can be used within a main tag, a section tag, or an article. The use of the footer element is to place it at the bottom of a document to contain things like a notice copyright, links to related content, other information about the owner of the website.

DOCTYPE

The declaration of <!DOCTYPE html> is used to inform the web visitor's browser that the document being rendered is an HTML document. Although not actually an HTML element per se, every HTML document should come with a DOCTYPE declaration to conform to HTML standards.

```
<html lang="en">
  <head>
    <meta charset="UTF-8" />
    <meta http-equiv="X-UA-Compatible"
content="IE=edge" />
    <meta  content="width=device-width, initial-
scale=1.0" name="viewport" />
    <title>Footer Using Html Css</title>
    <link
      href="https://cdn.jsdelivr.net/npm/
bootstrap@5.1.3/dist/css/bootstrap.min.css"
```

```
      rel="stylesheet"
    />
    <link
      rel="stylesheet"
 href="https://cdnjs.cloudflare.com/ajax/libs/font-
awesome/6.1.1/css/all.min.css"
    />
    <style>

* {
    margin: 0;
    padding: 0;
    box-sizing: border-box;
    color: #fff;

}
h1{
  text-align: center;
  padding:30px
}
a,
a:hover,
a.focus,
a.active {
    text-decoration: none;
    outline: none;
}

ul {
    margin: 0;
    padding: 0;
    list-style: none;
}

li a{
  text-decoration:none;
}

.footer {
    background: linear-gradient(105deg, rgb(154, 12,
72), #a129a5);
}
```

```css
.footer_section h4,
.social_media h4 {
    color: #fff;
    margin-top: 0;
    margin-bottom: 25px;
    font-weight: 700;
    text-transform: uppercase;
    font-size: 20px;
}

.footer_section h4::after,
.social_media h4::after {
    content: "";
    display: block;
    height: 2px;
    width: 40px;
    background: #fff;
    margin-top: 20px;
}

.footer_section ul {
    margin: 0;
    padding: 0;
    list-style: none;
}

.footer_section ul li a {
    color: #fff;
    transition: all .3s ease 0s;
    line-height: 36px;
    font-size: 15px;
    text-transform: capitalize;
}

.footer_section ul li a:hover {
    color: #f1f1f1;
}

.footer_section_contact ul li {
    color: #fff;
}
```

```
.search form {
    width: 100%;
    position: relative;
    display: flex;
    margin-bottom: 10px;
    box-shadow: rgba(149, 157, 165, 0.2) 0px 8px 24px;
}

.contact_input {
    width: 100%;
    border: none;
    padding: 0 0 0 15px;
    height: 60px;
    border-radius: 5px 0 0 5px;
    outline: none;
    color: #999;
    font-size: 16px;
}

.submit_button {
    width: 70px;
    height: 60px;
    font-size: 20px;
    border: none;
    background: #fff;
    text-align: center;
    color: #e1a0ee;
    border-radius: 0 5px 5px 0;
    cursor: pointer;
}

.social_media ul{
    display: flex;
    justify-content: space-between;
}

.social_media ul li {
    text-align: center;
    line-height: 50px;
    font-size: 16px;
    width: 50px;
    height: 50px;
    border-radius: 50%;
```

```
      border: 1px solid #a129a5;
      background-color: #a129a5;
      transition: all .5s ease;
}

.social_media ul li:hover {
      border: 1px solid #a129a5;
      background-color: transparent;
}

.social_media ul li a {
      font-weight: 100;
      color: #fff;
}

@media screen and(max-width:400px) {
      .footer {
           padding: 0 10px;
      }
}
    </style>
  </head>
  <body>
    <div class="footer pt-5">
      <h1> Footer </h1>
      <div class="container">
        <div class="row">
          <div class="col-6 col-sm-6 col-md-4 col-lg-3
mb-5">
              <div class="footer_section">
                <h4>Links</h4>
                <ul>
                  <li><a href="#"> Link 1 </a></li>
                  <li><a href="#"> Link 2 </a></li>
                  <li><a href="#"> Link 3 </a></li>
                  <li><a href="#"> Link 4 </a></li>
                </ul>
              </div>
            </div>
            <div class="col-6 col-sm-6 col-md-4 col-lg-3
mb-5">
              <div class="footer_section">
                <h4>Guides</h4>
```

```
            <ul>
              <li><a href="#"> Link 1 </a></li>
              <li><a href="#"> Link 2 </a></li>
              <li><a href="#"> Link 3 </a></li>
              <li><a href="#"> Link 4 </a></li>
            </ul>
          </div>
        </div>
        <div class="col-6 col-sm-6 col-md-4 col-lg-3
mb-5">
          <div class="footer_section">
            <h4>Projects</h4>
            <ul>
              <li><a href="#"> Link 1 </a></li>
              <li><a href="#"> Link 2 </a></li>
              <li><a href="#"> Link 3 </a></li>
              <li><a href="#"> Link 4 </a></li>
            </ul>
          </div>
        </div>
        <div class="col-12 col-sm-6 col-md-12
col-lg-3 mb-5">
          <div class="row">
            <div
              class="col-sm-12 col-md-6 col-lg-12
footer_section footer_section_contact"
            >
              <h4>Contact Us</h4>
              <div class="search">
                <form action="#" class="subscribe">
                  <input
                    type="email"
                    class="contact_input"
                    placeholder="E-mail address"
                  />
                  <button type="submit"
class="submit_button">
                    <i class="fa fa-paper-plane">
</i>
                  </button>
                </form>
              </div>
```

```
            </div>
           </div>
          </div>
         </div>
       </div>
     </div>
   </body>
</html>
```

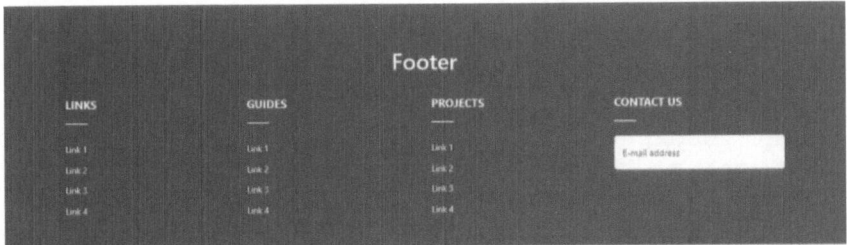

Footer in HTML.

HTML Document Template

The below template shows how all these elements are properly nestled within each other. You can use it as a standard template for all your HTML documents.

```
<!DOCTYPE html>
<html lang="en">
<head>
    <title> HTML </title>
    <style>
        body{
            text-align: center;
            margin:0;
            padding:10px;
            font-size: 20px;
        }
          header{
border:1px solid darkblue;
height:100px;
margin: 2px;
}
```

```
nav{
    border:1px solid darkblue;
height:120px;
margin: 2px;

}
main{
height:200px;
display:flex;
flex-direction: row;

}
.section1{
height:200px;
width:80%;
display:flex;
flex-direction: column;

}
section{
    border:1px solid darkblue;
    height:120px;
    flex-direction: row;
margin: 2px;

}

article{
    border:1px solid darkblue;
    height:140px;
    flex-direction: row;
    margin: 2px;

}
aside{
    border:1px solid darkblue;
    width:30%;
    margin: 2px;
}
.section2{
  display:flex;
  flex-direction:row;
```

```
      border:1px solid darkblue;
height:100px;
margin: 2px;

}
footer{
  width:50%;
  float: right;
}

address{
  width:50%;
  float: right;
}

    </style>
  </head>
<body>
  <h1> HTML Structure </h1>
    <header>
        Header Tag Content
    </header>
    <nav>
        Navbar Tag Content
    </nav>
    <main>
        <div class="section1">
            <section>
                Section Tag Content
            </section>
            <article>
                Article  Tag Content
            </article>
        </div>
  <aside>
        Aside Tag Content
    </aside>
    </main>
    <div class="section2">
      <footer>
        Footer Tag Content
    </footer>
```

```
<address>
  Address Tag Content
</address>
</div>
</body>
</html>
```

Use Lowercase Letters
Your HTML markup can also be written in lowercase or uppercase on the web page will render correctly.[11] However, it is recommended to keep tag names in lowercase letters as they are easier to read and maintain.

Reduce the Number of Elements on the Page
HTML documents can get complicated, especially for websites with a lot of content. To reduce the size of your pages, look for opportunities to further optimize your code once you've completed markup.

Validate Frequently
Instead of waiting until you're done with your HTML document, check your code multiple times as you work. This will help you save time at the end by identifying errors early, especially if your document is long. One of the popular HTML validators to use is the W3C Tag Validation Service.

Always Place the External Stylesheets in the <head> Tag
Although the external stylesheets can be placed anywhere in an HTML document, the best practice is to place them inside the <head> tag. This will make your page load faster.

Use Div Elements to Divide Your Layout into Main Sections
Consider dividing your website into main sections as the first step in creating a website design. It supports clean and well-indented code from the start. It also helps to avoid confusion and overuse of divs, especially if you write complex and long tags.

Example:

```
<div class="section1">
    <div class="content">
            Content
        </div>
```

```
        <div class="content">
          Content
        </div>
      <div class="content">
        Content
    </div>
      <div class="content">
        Content
    </div>
  </div>
</div>
```

Minify, Unify, and Shift JavaScript

Like CSS, never use inline JavaScript, try to minify and unify JavaScript libraries to reduce the HTTP requests that need to be made to generate one of your web pages. But unlike CSS, there's one really bad thing about external JavaScript files: browsers don't allow parallel downloads, which means the browser can't download anything while the JavaScript is downloading, resulting in the page feeling like it's loading slowly. So the best strategy is to load JavaScript last (i.e. after loading your CSS). To do this, place the JavaScript at the end of the HTML document if possible. Best practice recommends doing this just before the final <body> tag.

Example:

```
  </body>
  <link rel="stylesheet" href="http://ajax.
googleapis.com/ajax/libs/jqueryui/1.8.9/themes/
base/jquery-ui.css" type="text/css" media="all" />
  <script src="http://ajax.aspnetcdn.com/ajax/
jQuery/jquery-1.5.min.js" type="text/
javascript"></script>
  <script src="http://ajax.googleapis.com/ajax/libs/
jqueryui/1.8.9/jquery-ui.min.js" type="text/
javascript"></script>
  </html>
```

Use Heading Elements Wisely

Learn how to use the <h1> to <h6> elements to mark the hierarchy of HTML content. This will make content more meaningful to screen readers and search engines, as well as other users.

Example:

```
<h1>This is the top heading</h1>
<h2>This is the subheading under the top
heading.</h2>
<h3>This is the subheading under the h2
heading.</h3>
```

Use the Right HTML Element in the Right Place
Familiarize yourself with all present HTML elements and use them correctly for semantic and meaningful content structure. It uses <em> for emphasis and <strong> for strong emphasis instead of <i> or <b>.

Don't Use divs for Everything
Sometimes developers end-up wrapping <div> tags around multiple <div> tags that contain multiple <div> tags, creating a mountain of divs. According to the latest draft of the W3C HTML specification, <div> is a meaningless element that is used "as an element for last resort when no other element is suitable". But many also use it for menial things like displaying inline elements as block elements (instead of the display:block; CSS property). Avoid creating mountains of wonders by using them sparingly and responsibly.

Use an Unordered List (<ul>) for Navigation
Navigation is a very important aspect of website design, and the <ul> element combined with CSS makes your navigation menus semantic. By convention, an unordered list is also an accepted notation for your navigation menu.

Use Alternate Attributes with Images
Using a meaningful alt attribute with <img> elements is a must for writing valid and semantic code.

Example:

```
<img src="https://images.pexels.com/
photos/8581948/pexels-photo-8581948.jpeg?auto=comp
ress&cs=tinysrgb&w=600&lazy=load" alt=" Beach " />
```

Avoid Excessive Comments

The purpose of documenting code is to make it easier to understand, so commenting out code logic is a good thing for programming languages like PHP, Java, and C#. But markup is self-explanatory and commenting every line of code doesn't make sense in HTML/XHTML. If you find commenting your HTML a lot to explain what's going on, you should check your work for semantics and appropriate naming conventions.

Choose a Great Code Editor

Now there are tons of great code editors you can use, from something basic and lightweight like Notepad++ to full-fledged IDEs. It's free, built on open source, and comes with tons of extensions to help you write better code faster. There are also many code editors available, such as Atom, Brackets, and Vim. Just choose the one you like the most and start coding.

Start Using the New HTML5 Tags

In the earlier days, different parts of a page were wrapped in div tags. That is why there was no way to give page a more semantic structure. It comes with a lot of various new tags that we can use to structure the content on our website. This includes tags like navigation, section, article, aside, etc.

One h1 Per Page

Use only one h1 per page. Put the important text that describes the content of the page. For example, your blog post or article title. Using multiple h1 tags per page is not necessarily a good idea and is not recommended as it can harm your search engine results. It helps search engines to index site in the right way. It is also defined in the W3C specifications and the content of your page should be described by a single tag in any case.

Stop Supporting IE

Whatever comments or tags you add to your HTML to support IE, just stop! If you don't have to strictly build for this browser, try recommending other browsers to this user instead of adding some horrible thing to your markup for IE.

Always Specify the Button Type

A simple rule! Always specify the button type. By default, the button is of type "submit", which is not always the desired behavior. As a general rule, always be clear about the type of things you want, even if it's the default.

Example:

```
<button type="button">My Button</button>
<input type="text"/>
```

Using Title Attributes with Links (If Needed)
Using the title attribute in anchor elements will improve accessibility when used in the right way. It is good to understand that the title attribute should be used to enhance the importance of the anchor tag.

BEST CODING PRACTICES

1. Start with DOCTYPE
   DOCTYPE is required for activating mode.

   ```
   <!DOCTYPE html>

   <html>
      . . .
   </html>
   ```

2. Don't use XML declaration.

   ```
   <!DOCTYPE html>
   ```

3. Do not use character references as much as possible.
   If you write an HTML document with UTF-8, almost all characters can be written directly such as:

   ```
   <p> <small> Copyright © 2014 <sup> ® </sup>
   </small> </p>
   ```

4. Escape &, <, >, ", and ' with named character references.
   These characters should escape always for a bug-free HTML document.

   ```
   <h1>The &quot; &amp; &quot; character</h1>
   Result  = The "&" character
   ```

5. Put white spaces around comment contents.
   Some characters cannot be used immediately after comment open or before comment close.
   ```
   <!-- This section is non-normative -->
   ```

6. Don't mix empty element format. It should be consistent.

```
<img alt="HTML Best Practices" src="/img/logo.
png">
 <hr>
```

7. Don't omit closing tag.

```
<html>
  <body>
    . . .
  </body>
</html>
```

8. Don't mix character cases. It gives a consistency also.

```
<a href="#general">General</a>
```

SECURITY AND HARDENING IDEAS (HTML SECURITY)

It is commonly used for securing HTML Code and Content.[12] HTML security consists of three different security measures:

- HTML encryption to ensure that web content cannot be accessed by unauthorized users.

- Using digital certificates to verify the domain and ensure that the content comes from a trusted location (the URL in the browser's address bar).

- Encrypting content on its way from the server to the client and back (SSL).

Security is a topic that comes up from time to time. It's not a problem from the start, but once something bad happens, it's usually blamed. The software is complex, the human programming of the machine is far from perfect, and the user may not follow the best practices either. So this is how we can create a secure system.

The web is one of the most dangerous places possible. Computers with potential security risks are interconnected. Servers can receive any data. Clients run code from unknown sources. While we cannot control the security of servers, we must do something to protect clients. While

JavaScript might be considered a safe scripting language, the code for any ActiveX, Flash, or Silverlight plugins certainly isn't. Additionally, even if JavaScript itself is sandboxed, it can be used in such a way that the user triggers insecure actions.

SECURITY

One of the most necessary guidelines has nothing to do with HTML directly: Use HTTPS![13] The relation to HTML is, of course, in the distribution of our hypertext documents. However, we must remember that using HTTPS to transfer our documents and using HTTPS for our resources are two different things. It is definitely necessary to check that all contained resources are actually using the https:// scheme.

Another important guideline concerns user-defined content. Once we allow users to enter data into a form, we need to be careful. Not only do we need to make sure that the web server is protected against common attacks like SQL injection, we also need to make sure that stored data is not used in executable code without care. For example, we should not have any HTML escape strings. The HTML itself is not malicious, but it can cause a script to run or resources to be loaded. The only way to allow users to write HTML that will be placed on the output page without modification is to whitelist certain tags and attributes. Other elements will be leaked.

Our JavaScripts should also minimize exposure and reliance on third-party libraries. Of course, we use the immediately invoke function expression (IIFE) to avoid polluting the global context; however, another reason is to avoid leaking (probably) crucial internal states that can then be intentionally or accidentally changed by other scripts.

It is certainly good practice for ourselves to rely on "strict usage"; and mediated benefits. However, limiting the running script does not prevent us from using the API with potentially corrupted data. Cookies and content in local storage may be changed or displayed by the user or other programs depending on conditions beyond our control. Therefore, we should always have some sanity checks in place to help us detect integrity flaws as early as possible. We should make sure that we only use trusted third-party sources. The use of scripts from other servers within our website can change the page or violate the privacy of our users.

METHODS OF COMMUNICATION IN HTML

There is also a well-associated JavaScript API in HTML5. Also, new technologies open up the way we communicate between client and server and across documents. Let's look.

- XHR and XHR2 with CORS

- Web news

- Web sockets

- Events sent by the server

- Web Workers

Common Communication Event Model (XHR)

All event handlers receive an event object containing a date property. This property includes the sent data as part of the message. The event model is mostly based on onmessage and postMessage or send.

Example:

```
<script>
  // in the recipient code
recipient.onmessage = function (event) {
  console.log(' Message Received: ' + event.data);
};

// from the sender code
recipient.postMessage(' Hi there'); // or it can
be recipient.send('Hi there');
</script>
```

This is a common model and is not exactly the same between all these technologies. The two similarities are that they use:

- sending method (postMessage or send) on the receiver object and

- an event handler listens for message events and receives an event object containing the date property.

```
<Script>
  window.onmessage = function (event) {
  if (event.origin == 'mytrustedsite.com') {
    alert('my trusted site said: ' + event.data);
  }
};
</Script>
```

Support for postMessage:

- Chrome

- Safari

- Opera

- Firefox

- IE8

Web Sockets

Web sockets are also used to send messages to and from the server – i.e. a two-way socket. Unlike other similar technologies, with Web Sockets you can browse across domains and are not bound by same-origin policies. This means you can host your normal "app" server while another server is used for streaming contentYou can only send messages when the socket is open (duh). The communication model looks like this:

```
<Script>

var vas = new WebSocket('ws://somesite.com/updates');

vas.onmessage = function (event) {
  alert(event.data);
};

vas.onopen = function () {
  vas.send('yay! we connected!');
};
</Script>
```

Support for Web Sockets

- Chrome

- Safari and MobileSafari

Server-Sent Events

The Server-Sent Events API is used to send events from the server to the client. The client can't send messages to the server via EventSource (SSE). It can only listen to messages.

The API uses the onmessage model. It is created using an EventSource object and is constrained by the same origin rules:

```html
<script>
  var es = new EventSource('/sse');
  es.onopen = function () {
    console.log('opened stream');
  };

  es.onmessage = function (event) {
    console.log('new message: ' + event.data);
  };
</script>
```

Web Workers

Web Workers are a way to create a new thread of execution inside the browser. It includes communicating with web workers and the way you communicate is similar to some of the techniques above. However, everyone should be aware that this is not a method of communication from the client (browser) to the server. It's more like there's another browser window that executes a specific block of JavaScript.

For Example, if you're using a lot of JavaScript and the UI becomes unresponsive. The browser UI gets stuck because it's a "single-threaded application" in a way. The JavaScript task can be outsourced to the web worker so that the user interface can continue to function.

Web Messaging

Web Messaging is mainly used to share data by separating the browser context without using the DOM and overcomes the problems in cross-domain communication across different domains, protocols, or ports.[14]

Instead of sending data from the user's page, you can just add content that is present in a frame or vice versa, where the browser sends a security alert instead of a message event.

Web Messaging Events
The web messaging events are used in action for cross-document messaging, channel messaging, server-sent events, and web sockets. It has described by Message Event interface.

- data: It is used to store the string data.
- origin: It is used to store the domain name and port.
- source: It is used to store an originating document window.
- ports: It is used to store the data that is sent by any message port.
- lastEventId: It is used to store the unique identifier of the current message event.

Sending a Message across Documents
Before sending a message between documents, we need to create a new web browsing context by creating either a new iframe or a new window. We can send the data using postMessage() and it has two arguments such as:

- message – The message to send
- targetOrigin – Origin name

HTML5 Channel Messages
Channel Messaging is used for the browsing context, which is a two-way communication commonly used for multiple resources. If you want to create a message, it internally creates two separate ports that are used for sending and forwarding to another browser context as shown below:

- postMessage() – It is used to post a message using a channel.
- start() – It is used to send data.
- close() – It is used to close ports.

Cross-Origin Resource Sharing (CORS)
The concept of CORS is simple. The browser does not allow embedding of special resources from different sources unless the origins explicitly allow

it. For example, special resources can be web fonts or anything requested via XMLHttpRequest. AJAX requests from various sources are disabled by default due to their ability to make advanced requests that introduce many scripting security issues. The origin is basically defined by the combination of protocol, host, and port used.

Clients can allow to use resources by including some headers in the response. The browser then determines whether or not the current web page can use the resource. The origin is usually determined using the domain of the current website.

Let's look at an illustrative example. We further assume that our site is located at foo.com. We request JSON data from a page hosted on bar.com. For JSON request, we use XMLHttpRequest as shown below.

```
<script>
  var es = new EventSource('/sse');
  var xhr = new XMLHttpRequest();
xhr.open('GET', 'https://bar.com/users');
xhr.addEventListener('load', function (ev) {
    if (xhr.status === 200) {
        var result = JSON.parse(xhr.responseText);
        // ...
    }
}, false);
xhr.send();
  </script>
```

The browser already assumes a CORS-enabled response option by adding an Origin header to the request such as:

```
Origin: http://foo.com
```

Now the server must deliver the correct response. Not only do we want the correct JSON to be transported, but more importantly we require specific CORS headers. The following example will grant the right to use the requested resource for any request.

```
Access-Control-Allow-Origin: *
```

CORS can also be used as an alternative to JSONP solutions. JSONP uses scripts to make AJAX requests from various sources that result in JSON responses. Before CORS, cross-domain calls were generally forbidden, but including scripts from different domains was always acceptable. In most APIs, a JSONP response was triggered by providing a special query parameter that named the callback function.

Suppose the call to "http://bar.com/api" results in the following JSON response such as:

```
{ "name": "example", "factor": 5, "active": true }
```

The JSONP call to, e.g., http://bar.com/api?jsonp=setResult would give us:

```
setResult({ "name": "example", "factor": 5, "active":
true });
```

Since only the <script> element sees the JSONP result, the GET request method is assumed. There is no option to use anything else. CORS gives us much more freedom in this area, so we can specify other parameters as well. All of this is made possible by allowing us to freely use the standardized XMLHttpRequest object.

Sandboxing Flags

Each document has its own window. Access to this window is usually through the proxy window of the current browsing context, which controls the tab we see. A browsing context is created with several options such as parent context, creator, and splash page. Security flags are set along with these options. Flags set the options and constraints of the context. In fact, it is possible to prevent certain behaviors such as running scripts or opening new tabs.

There are a bunch of flags available. The most important ones are such as:

- allow-top-navigation (it allows changing the top context)
- allow-plugins (it enables embed, object, ...)
- allow-same-origin (its content from the same origin may be accessed)
- allow-forms (its forms can be submitted)
- allow-popups (its popups/new contexts won't be blocked)
- allow-pointer-lock (it enables the pointer-lock API)
- allow-scripts (it allows script execution)

CHAPTER SUMMARY

In this chapter, we have discussed various points and by using them, you can improve your code writing in HTML.

NOTES

1. HTML Code – https://www.keycdn.com/blog/frontend-optimization, accessed on September 6, 2022.
2. HTML Code – https://www.keycdn.com/blog/frontend-optimization, accessed on September 6, 2022.
3. HTML Code – https://www.keycdn.com/blog/frontend-optimization, accessed on September 6, 2022.
4. Code Optimization – https://www.imperva.com/learn/performance/front-end-optimization-feo/, accessed on September 6, 2022.
5. Code Optimization – https://www.imperva.com/learn/performance/front-end-optimization-feo/, accessed on September 6, 2022.
6. Code Optimization – https://one-inside.com/optimize-front-end-performance/, accessed on September 7, 2022.
7. Code Optimization – https://one-inside.com/optimize-front-end-performance/, accessed on August 7, 2022.
8. Prefetch and Reload in HTML – https://www.digitalocean.com/community/tutorials/html-preload-prefetch, accessed on September 7, 2022.
9. Code Optimization – https://javascript.plainenglish.io/15-useful-techniques-you-can-use-to-improve-your-frontend-optimization-8317cb6e54e9, accessed on September 7, 2022.
10. HTML Coding Tip – https://html.com/document/, accessed on September 8, 2022.
11. HTML Coding Tips – https://blog.tbhcreative.com/2015/08/10-best-practices-in-html.html, accessed on September 8, 2022.
12. Security in HTML – https://www.locklizard.com/html-security/, accessed on September 9, 2022.
13. Security in HTML – https://code.tutsplus.com/tutorials/html5-mastery-web-security--cms-24846, accessed on September 9, 2022.
14. HTML Web Messaging – https://tutorials.freshersnow.com/html5/html5-web-messaging/, accessed on September 9, 2022.

HTML for Game Development

IN THIS CHAPTER

➢ Building block HTML

➢ HTML5 Game Development

The previous chapter was all about the code optimization. Here in this chapter, we will start our new topic – Game development in HTML.

Let's start from scratch.[1] What is HTML? There is a good definition of HTML5, which simply means the latest revision of HTML (the markup language used around the world to create web pages), and a more hyped definition (what most people understand when they say HTML5), which is the "new" features of web technologies that appeared in the last few years (JavaScript APIs like Canvas or WebAudio, semantic HTML tags, etc.).

For our purpose, we will use pieces of these two. HTML5 is the latest version, which includes a whole host of great features that make web technologies an open standard with endless possibilities for combining HTML, CSS, and JavaScript.

HTML along with all these superpowers that go beyond a simple web allows us to create games among other things. This is an HTML5 game.

DOI: 10.1201/9781003357537-4

BUILDING BLOCKS

Essentially, HTML code looks just like regular text.[2] A great feature of HTML code is the use of curly braces. These curly braces enclose markup code that tells the browser how to display the document's data.

Example:

```
<!DOCTYPE html>
<head>
  <title>Page Title</title>
</head>

<body>
  <h1> This is a heading. </h1>
  <p> This is a paragraph. </p>
</body>
</html>
```

Above are the basics of what a website consists of. If you've ever wanted to know what the page you're on looks like in HTML form, switch the page to source mode. Switching a page to source mode can seem very scary with a lot of coding involved. However, once you understand the fundamentals of HTML, it's easy to see how it all works. If you want to fully understand the basics of coding, you need to know the three building blocks: tags, elements, and attributes.

Tags

The pieces of text that can be found inside curly braces along with square brackets are called "tags". It is used to separate code from normal text. They also help tell the browser how to display the web page between the opening and closing tags. These two are: <html> and </html>. Some tags come in pairs as one tag is used to open the tag and the other to close it, the difference is shown in the HTML tags above. Finally, you should always remember to open and close labels and remember to use angle brackets to make them work.

Elements

Elements are a tag as a whole, so this includes the opening tag, the text inside, and then the closing tag as well. Subsequently, the web page is made up of many HTML elements, all of which are put together like a giant puzzle. The elements are very easy to understand once you understand the tags. The only part of elements where it can be tricky is when elements appear within elements, but if you practice this section a lot you'll find it's not difficult as long as you know where to put the element codes.

Attributes

These are used to define more specific information within an element. They usually come in pairs name and value (name="value"). Attributes can also be used to facilitate resizing images, changing the font, size, and color of text. This means that most element types will only appear/use when we need them. The main two points you'll need to remember about attributes are to enclose the value in quotes to make it easier to identify. Second, write it in lowercase letters.

The basic building blocks of an HTML5 game are those from the web, such as:

- HTML

- CSS

- JavaScript

Similar to HTML5, when people talk about CSS3 they're usually referring to the new stuff that comes with the latest CSS specs, but by analogy, CSS3 is simply the latest CSS. Ignoring the semantics of these definitions for a moment and thinking about the hyped versions of these terms, we may also need to make HTML5 games:

- HTML5 (JavaScript API)

- CSS3

With the above, you can create amazing games that will run in modern web browsers on mobile and desktop, but sometimes games may require more features, so you can add more building blocks.

For example, you might want to create 3D games. If that's the case, there's also WebGL, which is a JavaScript API for rendering 2D and 3D graphics in the browser using the GPU for higher performance.

HTML5 GAME FUNDAMENTALS

Although browser games are often called "HTML5 games", they require more than just HTML5 to function properly.[3] The HTML5 prefix refers to the use of the canvas element for game development. Now, all major browsers support canvas, which is why it is usually considered the best choice.

Items in the canvas element can be generated programmatically or loaded as graphics. Sometimes HTML5 games rely on sprites and tileable patterns, very similar to old SNES and Game Boy titles. More advanced graphics can be rendered using the WebGL/3D libraries, but most people just starting to learn and practice game development prefer 2D for its simplicity.

A web game breaks down into an HTML document with a canvas element for interaction. The canvas contains assets/sprites for characters, enemies, treasure chests, etc. Most of these graphics can be loaded using CSS. Computer games rely on mouse clicks or keystrokes for user interaction. The reliable way to handle this interaction is with JavaScript. Once the canvas screen is set up, most developers work to implement the functionality in JavaScript or a JS library.

HTML5 essentially replaced Flash game development with a broader API and more public support. Older versions of IE do not support canvas, so you'll either have to resign yourself to that demographic or try using an add-on library like ExploreCanvas.

DEFINING GOALS FOR GAME DEVELOPMENT

Before writing a line of code, it would be beneficial to plan the design of your game.[4] Write (or write) a general guide for the purpose of the game, how users play, and what defines "winning" the game.

Whether you're building a puzzle or a sidescroller, game mechanics are important. Some events will need to be programmed in JavaScript to respond when players reach something – or don't reach something.

HTML5, CSS3, and JavaScript all work well together and they can be used to create fun gaming experiences. But the mechanics are still new, so it's good to have your ideas planned well in advance. Think of a list of necessary features and how those features would be coded. If you want to build game like a player who lose their life and have to restart the game, how do you show scores? Also, think about interacting with the user in terms of how they would feel "most comfortable" while playing the game.

User Interaction Processing

Interactive components are what that define games.[5] A game without an active player is just a pretty graphic on the screen. It is the way to handle user actions, both from the mouse and from the keyboard.

JavaScript has built-in methods for capturing interactions known as event listeners. It can be set to listen and record whenever an event occurs, such as a mouse click or the "A" key being pressed. Once this happens, the event listener can fire the function and do whatever you want.

More complex interactions can occur regardless of user input. For example, suppose you play game of Mario and when Mario walks into a turtle, what happens? He loses his life. If you were building a game clone of Mario, you would have to listen to this event and fire a function if the player hits the turtle.

However, not all games have to follow these templates. Take this word search game that runs like a typical crossword puzzle. It drag to highlight words and points are awarded based on the number of words solved.

The features and calculations for the word search game are significantly different compared to Super Mario. However, both require user interaction, which in the HTML5 gaming world relies heavily on JavaScript.

Server Side in an HTML5 Game

If you want your games to save data remotely, you will need a server side for your game. You can develop your own backend using any server side language, in this case you will need a server.

- PHP
- Java:
  - JavaScript (NodeJS)
  - Ruby
  - Python

Or you can use a third-party backend as a Service provider like Firebase. Some have free versions that you can use and will start charging you once you exceed certain limits. Some of these providers focus mainly on games; some are mostly designed for mobile applications, but can also be used for games.

Graphics and Sprite Sheets

Game developers refer to music, graphics, and animation cycles as assets. For canvas games, these assets should be created and stored locally on the game server. Interactive elements and noninteractive elements must be considered when organizing graphic items. For a small RPG, the interactive elements would be the player character along with enemies and treasure chests. Anything that can interact with other things on the screen should be considered interactive.

Noninteractive graphics are like backgrounds and tiles. The Photoshop and Illustrator are the perfect choices for creating these BG graphics and exporting them for use on the web.

If you are interested in making 3D. WebGL is basically a JavaScript library/API for rendering advanced graphics in the browser. You can try to design your graphics using CSS3 transforms, but this is much more restrictive.

When it comes to animation, you will want to put together a sprite sheet of the characters at different stages. Since JavaScript can use to move objects around the page, you don't always have to create unique animations from scratch. But if you like 2D graphics style, try practicing sprite animation tutorials to get basic concepts for 2D game animation.

HTML5 Game Frameworks

Most games share some concepts like sprites (graphics that represent enemies, players, and elements in your game), scenes or stages, animations, sound, loading graphics, etc.[6] Because most game developers want to focus on their actual game rather than creating this whole abstract layer, we recommend using HTML5 game frameworks.

HTML5 game frameworks and libraries containing building components that you can use to create your own games. These libraries are Open-Source projects created as well as maintained by people who want to contribute to the HTML5 gamedev environment. In many cases, they have created frameworks for their own games, and after realizing that other people would not only want to use them, but also contribute to them, release them as Open-Source code, so everyone wins.

Choosing which game engine to use is an important decision, so do your research properly before choosing. There is no matter what engine you choose, you will need to familiarize yourself with its code and inner workings to use it properly, so they shouldn't be treated like dump.

If you're making HTML5 games, it makes a lot of sense to start with some kind of game engine or framework. There are many free HTML5 game engines and frameworks out there, from the very minimal to the very complex. Below we will discuss some of the most popular HTML5 game frameworks as well as particle systems, game coding with code examples. For starters, we think it makes sense to take a step back and look at these HTML5 game development slides.

Amazing Facts about HTML5 Game Development
There are several ways to create an HTML5 game, and quite a bit of material on the technical side of each, so in this section we'll provide an overview of the benefits of HTML5 game development.

Multi-Platform

One of the most obvious advantages of HTML5 for games is that games will run on any modern device.[7] Yes, you will need to pay special attention to how your game will respond to different screen sizes and input types. We see too many games that don't work on mobiles and tablets, which is a really big mistake when developing any game, always keep mobile in mind when developing your HTML5 game.

You can create games that adapt to different requirements such as aspect ratios, screen size, resolution, etc. HTML5 games run not only on different platforms like iOS, Android, or Windows but also on browsers. HTML5 offers the ability to create games for different browsers and platforms. This means you only need to code once and you can deploy the game anywhere.

Unique Distribution

Most HTML5 games developed so far are built in the same way as Flash and native mobile games. This makes some sense, it overlooks the real benefits that the web as a platform adds.

HTML5 game distribution is often seen as a weakness, but that's only because we've looked at it in the same sense as native games, where the marketplace is the only way to find games. With HTML5 games, you have a powerful hyperlink. Links are thus easily distributed across the web and mobile devices.

Cleaner Code

Always keep your code clean.[8] HTML5 now makes it easier for you because any semantic and descriptive code can be written cleanly and separated in style form without any complex effort.

Geolocation API

Everything we can do in app, game development is about satisfying user needs. Using the HTML5 Geolocation API, you are able to automatically find where your user is in the world and ensure content is served to them. Of course, there are some issues with giving consent to track location, but given the benefits of browsing the web with geolocation turned on.

Makes Promotion Easier

HTML5 game development targets a wider audience because browsers of different operating systems support games developed using HTML5.[9] So whenever a developer creates a game, they can promote all the features once and for all through a simple website. Even sharing HTML5 games is a breeze. You can share any link to a website that players visit quite often and you're done. There are many websites dedicated specifically to HTML5 games.

Game Development Frameworks and Game Engines

A game engine is a framework or software development environment used to create games.[10] The game engines are one of the reasons game developers love developing HTML5 games.

HTML5 game engines take the tedious work out and make the game development process quite easy. Thus, developers need to spend less time creating a fully functional HTML5 game. They take care of game engines and frameworks:

- Audio
- Video
- Physics
- Maps
- Animations
- And more

All the above is necessary for creating puzzles, emulators, shooting, or poker games.

Phasers

Phaser is a game engine that you can use to create a game and compile it for different platforms. It is a cross-platform game engine that supports a wide variety of plugins, making it easy to develop HTML5 games. Submarine Dash, Elf Runner, Bayou Island are some of the popular games created with Phaser.

PlayCanvas WebGL Game Engine

The PlayCanvas game engine uses WebGL and HTML5 to run 3D content, including games, in desktop or mobile browsers. It's an open-source game engine, so anyone can add features to it.

If you want to develop or create 3D games using WebGL and HTML5 Canvas, PlayCanvas is the way to go. It is very powerful, optimized for mobile, and helps in faster game development. The Robostorm, Master Archer, Blast Arena, and Swoop are some of the games created with PlayCanvas.

Here is the various engine used for 2D html animations and games development:

- GDevelop
- Modd.io
- Construct 2
- ImpactJS Engine
- EaselJS
- Phaser
- pixi.js
- GameMaker
- Turbulenz
- lycheeJS
- CAAT
- melonJS
- Cocos2d-X
- WADE
- Quintus

- Crafty
- enchant.js
- LimeJS
- Isogenic Engine
- Panda.js
- Kiwi.js
- GC DevKit

Here is the various engine used for 3D html animations and games development:

- Construct 2
- BabylonJS
- Three.js
- Turbulenz
- voxel.js
- PlayCanvas

New HTML5 Features

The most important feature that was added to HTML5 is that it recognizes that the World Wide Web has a very definite structure.[11] There are many new tags and elements like navigation, aside, article, audio, video, canvas, etc. have been added in HTML5 to create a more structured website. Some of the new features are the semantic replacements and some provide new features. The most important new features are:

- A <canvas> element is added for designing and working with 2D graphics.
- Local storage, web storage, and multi-threading can also be done in HTML5 using web workers.
- Web Sockets are now fully HTML5 compliant, allowing two-way communication between parent and child pages on multiple domains.

- <Video> and <audio> tags were introduced to add multimedia elements to the page.

Principles of HTML5 Game Design

Visual effects in games define overall look, feel, and playability. Gamers are attracted by the high-visual quality that generates more traffic and reach. It is the key to creating successful games and provides a lot of fun for players. Here we would like to present some ideas on how to implement various visual effects in HTML5 games based on <canvas>. Before we get into it, now let's introduce the things we should learn before making game, such as:

- Basic game design that is used to create games and game effects such as game loops, sprites, collisions, and particle systems.

- The basic implementation of visual effects we will explore the theory and some code examples supporting these patterns.

Common Patterns

Let's start with some common patterns and elements used in game development:

- Sprites

- Sprite sheets

- Game loops

- Collision detection

- Particles and particle systems

- Euler integration

- Point

- Vector

Note that objects set in motion stay in motion. If you want to use some kind of deceleration to stop a moving object, you can use:

- Weapon effects

- Plasma

- Blaster

- Ray

- Rockets

- Flak

- Electro

HTML Canvas Graphics

Here, this section describes how to use the <canvas> element to draw 2D graphics, starting with the basics.[12] The examples provided should provide you a clear idea of what you can do with the canvas and provide code snippets that can help you get started with creating your own content.

A <canvas> is an HTML element that can be used to draw graphics using scripting (usually JavaScript). This can be used for example for drawing graphs, combining photos, or creating simple animations. The first introduced in WebKit by Apple for the macOS dashboard, <canvas> has since been implemented in browsers. Now, all major browsers support it.

Before the Start

Using the <canvas> element is not too difficult, but you need basic knowledge of HTML and JavaScript. The <canvas> element is not supported in older browsers but is supported in the latest versions of all major browsers. The default canvas size is 300 pixels × 150 pixels (width × height). However, custom sizes can be defined using the HTML height and width property. To draw graphics to the canvas, we use a JavaScript context object that creates graphics on the fly.

Basic Use of Canvas

The <canvas> tag is used to draw graphics on a web page. It displays four elements: a red rectangle, a gradient rectangle, a multi-colored rectangle, and a multi-colored text. Canvas can draw colored text, with or without animation. Canvas has great features for graphically presenting data with images of graphs and tables. Canvas can respond to JavaScript events. Canvas can respond to any user action (button click, mouse click, button click, finger movement). Animation canvas methods offer many possibilities for HTML game applications.

The "canvas" HTML element is used to draw graphics using JavaScript.[13] The "canvas" element is just a container for graphics. JavaScript should be used to draw the graphics. Canvas has several methods for drawing paths, frames, circles, text, and adding images. A canvas would be a rectangular area on an HTML page. By default, the canvas has no border or content.

Syntax:

```
<canvas>
  Content...
</canvas>
```

The <canvas> element basically is a container for graphics, you need a scripting language to draw graphics. The <canvas> element enables dynamic and scriptable rendering of 2D shapes and bitmap images.

It is a low-level procedural model that updates a bitmap and has no built-in scene. There are several methods in the canvas for drawing paths, frames, circles, text, and adding images.

The Canvas Element is officially a canvas that is "a resolution-dependent bitmap canvas that can be used for rendering charts, game graphics, or other visual images at runtime". Simply put, you can render 2D shapes and bitmap images using JavaScript and the HTML5 canvas element. The image below shows a canvas with a black border.

Example:

```
<!DOCTYPE html>
  <head>
    <title>Page Title</title>
  </head>
<body>
  <h2> Canvas HTML </h2>
    <canvas id="can" width="500" height="500"
style="border: 1px solid">
    </canvas>
</body>
</html>
```

The output of the code is given below.

Canvas HTML

Canvas border box.

In the above example, <canvas> looks like an <img> element the difference being that it doesn't have the src and alt attributes. In fact, the <canvas> element only has two attributes, width, and height. Both are optional and can also be set using DOM properties.

```
<!DOCTYPE html>
 <head>
   <title>Page Title</title>
   </head>
<body>
   <h2> Canvas HTML </h2>
    <canvas id="can" style="border: 1px solid">
    </canvas>
</body>
</html>
```

The output of the code is given below.

Canvas HTML

Canvas border box (no width and height given).

If no width and height attributes are specified, the canvas will initially be 300 pixels wide and 150 pixels high.

A web page can contain multiple canvas elements. Each canvas can have an ID that you can use to target a specific canvas via JavaScript. Each canvas element has a 2D context. This again has objects, properties, and methods. To draw on the canvas, you must reference the canvas context. The context gives you access to 2D properties and methods.

The id attribute is not specific to the <canvas> element but is one of the global HTML attributes that can be applied to any HTML element (such as a class).[14] It's always a good idea to include an ID as it makes it easier to identify in the script.

The <canvas> element can be styled like any normal image (border, border, background…). However, these rules do not affect the actual drawing on the canvas. We will see how it is done in the dedicated chapter of this tutorial. When no style rules are applied to the canvas, it will initially be fully transparent.

The <canvas> element requires a closing tag (</canvas>). If the tag is not present, the rest of the document will not be displayed. If you don't need fallback content, a simple <canvas id="foo" …> </canvas> is fully compatible with all browsers that support canvas at all.

About the <canvas> Tag
It is a graphic element. Use the HTML <canvas> element with either the canvas scripting API or the WebGL API to draw graphics and animations.

Using the class:[15]

- Classes (i.e. class names) are used to style the canvas element.

- Multiple class names are separated by a space.

- JavaScript uses classes to access elements by class name.

Syntax:

```
<canvas class="classname" >
```

A class attributes styling a <canvas> element. Every second, JavaScript toggles a classname that changes the border color.

Example:

```
<!DOCTYPE html>
 <head>
   <title>Page Title</title>
   <style>
 .bordered {border:4px solid lightblue;}
 .border-red { border-color: orangered; }
</style>
 </head>
<body>
  <h2> Canvas HTML (Change border color using
class) </h2>
  <canvas class="bordered" id="canvas"
  width="200" height="200"></canvas>

<script>

( () => {

let canvas = document.getElementById("canvas");
let context = canvas.getContext("2d");

context.fillStyle = "paleturquoise";
context.fillRect(22, 22, 150, 150);

setInterval( () => {
  canvas.classList.toggle("border-red");
```

```
}, 1000)

} ) ();

</script>
</body>
</html>
```

The output of the code is given below.

Canvas HTML (Change border color using class)

Canvas HTML (change border color using class).

Here is the description of the above code.

Two CSS classes are defined in the <style> element. A single class name is assigned to the class attribute in <canvas>. The JavaScript toggles another class and creates the impression of a flashing border. JavaScript uses an anonymous, self-executing lambda expression to start a process.

- The grid
- Drawing rectangles
- Drawing paths
- Drawing triangles
- Moving the pen
- Lines
- Arcs

- Bezier and quadratic curves

- Quadratic Bezier curves

- Rectangles

- Making a combination of shapes

- Path2D objects

- Using SVG paths

There are various shapes as you can see above all these shapes also have different methods such as to set any colors, styles, and shadows on the canvas, you can use these methods given below:[16]

- fillStyle: It sets or returns the color, gradient, or pattern used to fill the drawing.[17] The context.fillStyle is a property and not a method. A method is a function that we use to program the context to do something. For example, we program the context to draw a filled rectangle using the context.fillRect() method. When assigning a new color to the context.fillStyle property, we can manually assign the color ourselves. The context defines colors using CSS color values that are stored as text strings. There are several different ways to describe a color in CSS such as:

  1. Color names: Some specific colors have names that all web browsers can identify. For example, the context knows that context.fillStyle = 'DarkSalmon' actually means context.fillStyle = '#E9967A'. Here is the complete list of color names. We will discuss only some of them.

  2. Hexadecimal triplets: The color '#9932CC' is actually three separate numbers written in base 16. The first number (99) is the amount of red; the second number (32) is the amount of green; the third number (CC) is the amount of blue. The value for color components (red, green, and blue) can range from 00 (none) to FF (maximum).

  3. RGB values: To describe a color using RGB values, we use a string in the format: 'rgb(red, green, blue)'. The numbers 99, 32, CC in base-16 are equal to 153, 50, 204 in base-10, '#9931CC' & 'rgb(153, 50, 204)' both describe the same color. RGB values must be integers and range from 0 to 255.

4. RGBA format: A is Alpha values range from 0 to 1, where 0 is fully transparent and 1 is fully opaque. To set the fillStyle of the context to a dark orchid color that is 50% transparent, we use the text string "rgba(153, 50, 204, 0.5)" where the first three numbers are RGB values and the fourth number is alpha value.

Name	HEX Code	RGB Code
IndianRed	#CD5C5C	rgb(205, 92, 92)
LightCoral	#F08080	rgb(240, 128, 128)
Salmon	#FA8072	rgb(250, 128, 114)
DarkSalmon	#E9967A	rgb(233, 150, 122)
Pink	#FFC0CB	rgb(255, 192, 203)
LightPink	#FFB6C1	rgb(255, 182, 193)
HotPink	#FF69B4	rgb(255, 105, 180)
LightSalmon	#FFA07A	rgb(255, 160, 122)
Coral	#FF7F50	rgb(255, 127, 80)
Tomato	#FF6347	rgb(255, 99, 71)
Gold	#FFD700	rgb(255, 215, 0)
Yellow	#FFFF00	rgb(255, 255, 0)
LightYellow	#FFFFE0	rgb(255, 255, 224)
Lavender	#E6E6FA	rgb(230, 230, 250)
Thistle	#D8BFD8	rgb(216, 191, 216)
Plum	#DDA0DD	rgb(221, 160, 221)
Violet	#EE82EE	rgb(238, 130, 238)

Example:

```
<!DOCTYPE html>
 <head>
   <title>Page Title</title>
 </head>
 <body>
  <p> method using  - fillStyle() </p>
  <canvas id="myCanvas" width="500" height="500"
style="border:1px solid #d3d3d3;">
Your browser does not support the canvas element.
</canvas>

<script>
var canvas = document.getElementById('myCanvas');
var context = canvas.getContext('2d');
```

```
context.fillStyle = 'CornflowerBlue';
context.fillRect(20, 20, 100, 100); // First
rectangle

context.fillStyle = '#9932CC';
context.fillRect(80, 80, 100, 100); // Second
rectangle

context.fillStyle = 'rgb(255, 0, 0)';
context.fillRect(120, 140, 200, 100); // Third
rectangle

context.fillStyle = 'rgba(153, 50, 204, 0.5)';
context.fillRect(200, 100, 200, 100); // Fourth
rectangle

</script>
</body>
</html
```

method using - fillStyle()

Using method fillStyle().

The output of the code is given below.

- strokeStyle: It sets or returns the color, gradient, or pattern used for strokes.

Example:

```
<!DOCTYPE html>
 <head>
   <title>Page Title</title>
 </head>
 <body>

  <canvas id="myCanvas" width="300" height="300"
style="border:1px solid #d3d3d3;">
Your browser doesn't support the canvas element.
</canvas>

<script>
var c = document.getElementById("myCanvas");
var ctx = c.getContext("2d");
ctx.strokeStyle = "#FF0000";
ctx.strokeRect(20, 20, 150, 100);
</script>

</script>
</body>
</html
```

The output of the code is given below.

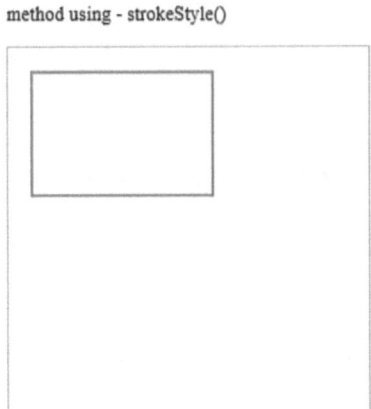

method using - strokeStyle()

Using method strokeStyle().

- shadowColor: It sets or returns the color to use for shadows.

- shadowBlur: It sets or returns the blur level for shadows.

Example:

```
<!DOCTYPE html>
 <head>
   <title>Page Title</title>
 </head>
 <body>
<h1> ShadowColor and ShadowBlur</h1>
  <canvas id="myCanvas" width="280" height="150"
style="border:1px solid #d3d3d3;">
Your browser doesn't support the canvas element.
</canvas>

<script>
var c = document.getElementById("myCanvas");
var ctx = c.getContext("2d");
ctx.shadowBlur = 20;
ctx.fillStyle = "lightgreen";

ctx.shadowColor = "black";
ctx.fillRect(20, 20, 100, 80);

ctx.shadowColor = "darkblue";
ctx.fillRect(140, 20, 100, 80);
</script>

</script>
</body>
</html
```

ShadowColor and ShadowBlur

Using method ShadowColor() and ShadowBlur().

- shadowOffsetX: It sets or returns the horizontal distance of the shadow from the shape.

- shadowOffsetY: It sets or returns the vertical distance of the shadow from the shape.

Example:

```
<!DOCTYPE html>
 <head>
   <title>Page Title</title>
 </head>
 <body>
<h1> shadowOffsetX and shadowOffsetY </h1>
  <canvas id="myCanvas" width="300" height="150"
style="border:1px solid #d3d3d3;">
Your browser doesn't support the canvas element.
</canvas>

<script>
var c = document.getElementById("myCanvas");
var ctx = c.getContext("2d");
ctx.shadowBlur = 20;
ctx.fillStyle = "pink";
ctx.shadowOffsetX = 20;
ctx.shadowOffsetY = 20;
ctx.shadowColor = "lightblue";
ctx.fillRect(20, 20, 100, 80);

ctx.shadowColor = "lightgreen";
ctx.fillRect(140, 20, 100, 80);
</script>

</script>
</body>
</html
```

Other methods:

- createLinearGradient(): It creates a linear gradient (for use on canvas content).

Example:

```
<!DOCTYPE html>
 <head>
```

```
   <title>Page Title</title>
  </head>
  <body>
<h1> createLinearGradient with all axis </h1>

<p> The x-coordinate of the start point of the
gradient </p>
   <canvas id="myCanvas_1" width="300"
height="150"
style="border:1px solid #d3d3d3;">
Your browser doesn't support the canvas element.
</canvas>

<p>The y-coordinate of the start point of the
gradient </p>
<canvas id="myCanvas_2" width="300" height="150"
style="border:1px solid #d3d3d3;">
Your browser doesn't support the canvas element.
</canvas>

<p> The x-coordinate of the end point of the
gradient </p>
<canvas id="myCanvas_3" width="300" height="150"
style="border:1px solid #d3d3d3;">
Your browser doesn't support the canvas element.
</canvas>

<p> The y-coordinate of the end point of the
gradient </p>
<canvas id="myCanvas_4" width="300" height="150"
style="border:1px solid #d3d3d3;">
Your browser doesn't support the canvas element.
</canvas>

<script>
var c = document.getElementById("myCanvas_1");
var ctx = c.getContext("2d");
var my_gradient = ctx.createLinearGradient(170,
0, 0, 0);

my_gradient.addColorStop(0, "black");
my_gradient.addColorStop(1, "white");
ctx.fillStyle = my_gradient;
ctx.fillRect(20, 20, 150, 100);
```

```
var c = document.getElementById("myCanvas_2");
var ctx = c.getContext("2d");
var my_gradient = ctx.createLinearGradient(0,
170, 0, 0);
my_gradient.addColorStop(0, "black");
my_gradient.addColorStop(1, "white");
ctx.fillStyle = my_gradient;
ctx.fillRect(20, 20, 150, 100);


var c = document.getElementById("myCanvas_3");
var ctx = c.getContext("2d");
var my_gradient = ctx.createLinearGradient(0, 0,
170, 0);
my_gradient.addColorStop(0, "black");
my_gradient.addColorStop(1, "white");
ctx.fillStyle = my_gradient;
ctx.fillRect(20, 20, 150, 100);

var c = document.getElementById("myCanvas_4");
var ctx = c.getContext("2d");
var my_gradient = ctx.createLinearGradient(0, 0,
0, 170);
my_gradient.addColorStop(0, "black");
my_gradient.addColorStop(1, "white");
ctx.fillStyle = my_gradient;
ctx.fillRect(20, 20, 150, 100);

</script>

</script>
</body>
</html
```

- createRadialGradient(): It creates a radial/circular gradient (for use on canvas content).

Example:

```
<!DOCTYPE html>
 <head>
   <title>Page Title</title>
 </head>
 <body>
<h1> createRadialGradient </h1>
```

```
  <canvas id="myCanvas" width="300" height="150"
style="border:1px solid #d3d3d3;">
Your browser doesn't support the canvas element.
</canvas>

<script>
var c = document.getElementById("myCanvas");
var ctx = c.getContext("2d");

var grd = ctx.createRadialGradient(74, 50, 5,
90, 60, 100);
grd.addColorStop(0, "blue");
grd.addColorStop(1, "lightgreen");

// Fill with gradient
ctx.fillStyle = grd;
ctx.fillRect(10, 10, 150, 100);
</script>

</script>
</body>
</html
```

- createPattern(): It repeats the specified element in the specified direction. The element can be an image, a video, or any other canvas element. Syntax is given below, context.createPattern(image, "repeat | repeat-x | repeat-y | no-repeat"):

  1. image: Specifies the image, canvas, or video element of the pattern to use.

  2. repeat: Repeats the pattern horizontally and vertically. It is the default.

  3. repeat-x: Repeats the pattern horizontally only.

  4. repeat-y: Repeats the pattern vertically only.

  5. no-repeat: Does not repeat the pattern.

Example:

```
<!DOCTYPE html>
<html>
<body>
```

```
<p>Image to use:</p>
<img src="https://images.pexels.com/
photos/9138500/pexels-photo-9138500.jpeg?auto=co
mpress&cs=tinysrgb&w=400&lazy=load" id="lamp"
width="32" height="32">
<p>Canvas:</p>

<button onclick="draw('repeat')">Repeat</button>
<button onclick="draw('repeat-x')">Repeat-x</
button>
<button onclick="draw('repeat-y')">Repeat-y</
button>
<button onclick="draw('no-repeat')">No-repeat</
button>

<canvas id="myCanvas" width="300" height="150"
style="border:1px solid #d3d3d3;">
Your browser doesn't support the HTML5 canvas
tag.</canvas>

<script>
function draw(direction) {
  var c = document.getElementById("myCanvas");
  var ctx = c.getContext("2d");
  ctx.clearRect(0, 0, c.width, c.height);
  var img = document.getElementById("lamp")
  var pat = ctx.createPattern(img, direction);
  ctx.rect(0, 0, 120, 130);
  ctx.fillStyle = pat;
  ctx.fill();
}
</script>

</body>
</html>
```

- addColorStop(): It specifies the stop colors and positions in the gradient object.

Example:

```
<!DOCTYPE html>
  <head>
    <title>Page Title</title>
  </head>
```

```
<body>
<h1> addColorStop  </h1>
  <canvas id="myCanvas" width="300" height="150"
style="border:1px solid #d3d3d3;">
Your browser doesn't support the canvas element.
</canvas>

<script>
var c = document.getElementById("myCanvas");
var ctx = c.getContext("2d");

var grd = ctx.createLinearGradient(0, 0, 170,
0);
grd.addColorStop(0, "black");
grd.addColorStop(1, "white");

ctx.fillStyle = grd;
ctx.fillRect(20, 20, 150, 100);
</script>

</script>
</body>
</html
```

To style line, you can use the following methods:

- lineCap: It sets or returns the style of the end caps for a line. There are three property values used to make a line:

  1. butt: It is default line. A flat edge is added to each end of the line

  2. round: A rounded end cap is added to each end of the line

  3. square: A square end cap is added to each end of the line

Example:

```
<!DOCTYPE html>
<html>
<body>

<p>The three different line caps:</p>
<canvas id="myCanvas" width="300" height="150"
style="border:1px solid #d3d3d3;">
```

Your browser doesn't support the HTML5 canvas
tag.</canvas>

```
<script>
var cn = document.getElementById("myCanvas");
var ctx = cn.getContext("2d");

ctx.beginPath();
ctx.lineWidth = 10;
ctx.lineCap = "butt";
ctx.moveTo(20, 20);
ctx.lineTo(200, 20);
ctx.stroke();

ctx.beginPath();
ctx.lineCap = "round";
ctx.moveTo(20, 40);
ctx.lineTo(200, 40);
ctx.stroke();

ctx.beginPath();
ctx.lineCap = "square";
ctx.moveTo(20, 60);
ctx.lineTo(200, 60);
ctx.stroke();
</script>

</body>
</html>
```

- lineJoin: It sets or returns the type of corner created when two lines meet. There are three property values used to make a line:

  1. bevel: It creates a beveled corner

  2. round: It creates a rounded corner

  3. miter: It is default and creates a sharp corner

Example:

```
<!DOCTYPE html>
<html>
<body>
```

```
<p>The three different line caps:</p>
<canvas id="myCanvas" width="300" height="150"
style="border:1px solid #d3d3d3;">
Your browser doesn't support the HTML5 canvas
tag.</canvas>

<script>
var cn = document.getElementById("myCanvas");
var ctx = cn.getContext("2d");
ctx.beginPath();
ctx.lineJoin = "round";
ctx.moveTo(20, 40);
ctx.lineTo(100, 70);
ctx.lineTo(20, 70);
ctx.stroke();
</script>

</body>
</html>
```

- lineWidth: It sets or returns the current line width.

Example:

```
<!DOCTYPE html>
<html>
<body>

<p>The three different line caps:</p>
<canvas id="myCanvas" width="300" height="150"
style="border:1px solid #d3d3d3;">
Your browser doesn't support the HTML5 canvas
tag.</canvas>

<script>
var cn = document.getElementById("myCanvas");
var ctx = cn.getContext("2d");
ctx.beginPath();
ctx.lineJoin = "round";
ctx.moveTo(20, 40);
ctx.lineTo(100, 70);
ctx.lineWidth = 5;
ctx.lineTo(20, 70);
```

```
ctx.stroke();
</script>
</body>
</html>
```

- miterLimit: It sets or returns the maximum miter length. It is of two types such as miter and bevel.

  1. Miter: If the miterLimit property is lineJoin attribute is "miter". The miterLimit property sets or returns the maximum miter length. It is the distance between the inner corner and the outer corner where two lines meet.

  2. Bevel: If the miter length exceeds the miterLimit value, the corner will be displayed as lineJoin type "bevel".

Example:

```
<!DOCTYPE html>
<html>
<body>

<p>The three different line caps:</p>
<canvas id="myCanvas" width="300" height="150"
style="border:1px solid #d3d3d3;">
Your browser doesn't support the HTML5 canvas
tag.</canvas>

<script>
var nc = document.getElementById("myCanvas");
var ctx = cn.getContext("2d");
ctx.beginPath();
ctx.lineJoin = "round";
ctx.moveTo(20, 40);
ctx.lineTo(100, 70);
ctx.lineWidth = 5;
ctx.lineTo(20, 70);
ctx.stroke();
</script>

</body>
</html>
```

To style rectangle, you can use the following methods:

- rect(): It creates a rectangle.

Example:

```
<!DOCTYPE html>
<html>
<body>

<p> Make rectangle using methods: rect() </p>
<canvas id="myCanvas_1" width="300" height="150"
style="border:1px solid #d3d3d3;">

Your browser doesn't support the HTML5 canvas
tag.</canvas>

<script>
var c = document.getElementById("myCanvas_1");
var ctx = c.getContext("2d");

// Red rectangle
ctx.beginPath();
ctx.lineWidth = "6";
ctx.strokeStyle = "yellow ";
ctx.rect(5, 5, 290, 140);
ctx.stroke();

ctx.beginPath();
ctx.lineWidth = "4";
ctx.strokeStyle = "green";
ctx.rect(30, 30, 50, 50);
ctx.stroke();

</script>

</body>
</html>
```

- fillRect(): It draws a "filled" rectangle.

Example:

```
<!DOCTYPE html>
<html>
<body>
```

```
<p> Make rectangle using methods: fillrect()
</p>
<canvas id="myCanvas_1" width="300" height="150"
style="border:1px solid #d3d3d3;">

Your browser doesn't support the HTML5 canvas
tag.</canvas>

<script>
var c = document.getElementById("myCanvas_1");
var ctx = c.getContext("2d");

ctx.fillRect(20, 20, 450, 100);
</script>
</body>
</html>
```

- strokeRect(): It draws a rectangle (no fill). It allows you to draw graphics on a web page using JavaScript. It has two elements that describe the height and width of the canvas, i.e. height and width respectively.

Example:

```
<!DOCTYPE html>
<html>
<body>

<p> Make rectangle using methods: strokeRect()
</p>
<canvas id="myCanvas_1" width="300" height="350"
style="border:1px solid #d3d3d3;">

Your browser doesn't support the HTML5 canvas
tag.</canvas>

<script>
var c = document.getElementById("myCanvas_1");
var ctx = c.getContext("2d");
ctx.strokeRect(120, 120, 120, 120);
</script>
</body>
</html>
```

- clearRect(): It clears the specified pixels within a given rectangle.

Example:

```
<!DOCTYPE html>
<html>
<body>

<p> Make rectangle using methods: clearRect()
</p>
<canvas id="myCanvas" width="300" height="350"
style="border:1px solid #d3d3d3;">

Your browser doesn't support the HTML5 canvas
tag.</canvas>

<script>
var cn=document.getElementById("myCanvas");
var ctx=cn.getContext("2d");
ctx.fillStyle="darkblue";
ctx.fillRect(0,0,300,150);
ctx.clearRect(20,20,100,50);
</script>
</body>
</html>
```

To style path, you can use the following methods:

- fill(): It fills the current drawing (path).

Example:

```
<!DOCTYPE html>
<html>
<body>

<p> Using methods: fill() </p>
<canvas id="myCanvas" width="300" height="350"
style="border:1px solid #d3d3d3;">

Your browser doesn't support the HTML5 canvas
tag.</canvas>
```

```
<script>
var c = document.getElementById("myCanvas");
var ctx = c.getContext("2d");

ctx.beginPath();
ctx.rect(20, 20, 150, 100);
ctx.fillStyle = "red";
ctx.fill();

ctx.beginPath();
ctx.rect(50, 40, 150, 100);
ctx.fillStyle = "blue";
ctx.fill();
</script>
</body>
</html>
```

- stroke(): It actually draws the path you have defined.

Example:

```
<!DOCTYPE html>
<html>
<body>

<p> Using methods: stroke() </p>
<canvas id="myCanvas" width="300" height="350"
style="border:1px solid #d3d3d3;">

Your browser doesn't support the HTML5 canvas
tag.</canvas>

<script>
var cn = document.getElementById("myCanvas");
   var ctx = cn.getContext("2d");
   ctx.beginPath();
   ctx.moveTo(100, 200);
   ctx.lineTo(100, 100);
   ctx.strokeStyle = "blue";
   ctx.stroke();
   ctx.beginPath();
   ctx.moveTo(30, 30);
```

```
    ctx.lineTo(20, 100);
    ctx.lineTo(170, 100);
    ctx.strokeStyle = "orange";
    ctx.stroke();
    </script>
</body>
</html>
```

- beginPath(): It begins a path, or resets the current path.

Example:

```
<!DOCTYPE html>
<html>
<body>

<p> Using methods: beginPath() </p>
<canvas id="myCanvas" width="300" height="350"
style="border:1px solid #d3d3d3;">

Your browser doesn't support the HTML5 canvas
tag.</canvas>

<script>
var cn = document.getElementById("myCanvas");
    var ctx = cn.getContext("2d");
    ctx.beginPath();
ctx.lineWidth = "5";
ctx.strokeStyle = "green"; // Green path
ctx.moveTo(10, 75);
ctx.lineTo(250, 75);
ctx.stroke(); // Draw it

ctx.beginPath();
ctx.strokeStyle = "purple"; // Purple path
ctx.moveTo(150, 0);
ctx.lineTo(150, 130);
ctx.stroke(); // Draw it
    </script>
</body>
</html>
```

- moveTo(): It moves the path to the specified point in the canvas, without creating a line.

Example:

```
<!DOCTYPE html>
<html>
<body>

<p> Using methods: moveTo() </p>
<canvas id="myCanvas" width="300" height="350"
style="border:1px solid #d3d3d3;">

Your browser doesn't support the HTML5 canvas
tag.</canvas>

<script>
var cn = document.getElementById("myCanvas");
   var ctx = cn.getContext("2d");
   ctx.beginPath();
ctx.lineWidth = "5";
ctx.strokeStyle = "green"; // Green path
ctx.moveTo(30, 75);
ctx.lineTo(250, 75);
ctx.stroke(); // Draw it

   </script>
</body>
</html>
```

- closePath(): It creates a path from the current point back to the starting point.

Example:

```
<!DOCTYPE html>
<html>
<body>

<p> Using methods: closePath() </p>
<canvas id="myCanvas" width="300" height="350"
style="border:1px solid #d3d3d3;">
```

```
Your browser doesn't support the HTML5 canvas
tag.</canvas>

<script>
var cv = document.getElementById("myCanvas");
var ctx = cv.getContext("2d");
ctx.beginPath();
ctx.moveTo(20, 20);
ctx.lineTo(20, 140);
ctx.lineTo(70, 140);
ctx.closePath();
ctx.stroke();

    </script>
</body>
</html>
```

- lineTo(): It adds a new point and creates a line to that point from the last specified point in the canvas.

Example:

```
<!DOCTYPE html>
<html>
<body>

<p> Using methods: lineTo() </p>
<canvas id="my_Canvas" width="300" height="350"
style="border:1px solid #d3d3d3;">

Your browser doesn't support the HTML5 canvas
tag.</canvas>

<script>
var cnv = document.getElementById("my_Canvas");
var ctx = cnv.getContext("2d");
ctx.beginPath();
ctx.moveTo(20, 20);
ctx.lineTo(20, 140);
ctx.lineTo(70, 140);
ctx.closePath();
ctx.stroke();
```

```
        </script>
    </body>
    </html>
```

- clip(): It clips a region of any shape and size from the original canvas.

Example:

```html
<!DOCTYPE html>
<html>
<body>

  <span>Without clip():</span>
  <canvas id="my_Canvas" width="300"
height="150" style="border:1px solid #d3d3d3;">
  Your browser doesn't support the HTML5 canvas
tag.</canvas>

  <script>
  var c = document.getElementById("my_Canvas");
  var ctx = c.getContext("2d");
  // Draw a rectangle
  ctx.rect(50, 20, 200, 120);
  ctx.stroke();
  // Draw red rectangle
  ctx.fillStyle = "grey";
  ctx.fillRect(0, 0, 150, 100);
  </script>
  <br> <br>
  <span>With clip():</span>
  <canvas id="my_Canvas2" width="300"
height="150" style="border:1px solid #d3d3d3;">
  Your browser doesn't support the HTML5 canvas
tag.</canvas>

  <script>
  var cnv = document.
getElementById("my_Canvas2");
  var ctx = cnv.getContext("2d");
  // Clip a rectangular area
  ctx.rect(50, 20, 200, 120);
  ctx.stroke();
  ctx.clip();
```

```
// Draw red rectangle after clip()
ctx.fillStyle = "grey";
ctx.fillRect(0, 0, 150, 100);
</script>

</body>
</html>
```

- quadraticCurveTo(): It creates a quadratic Bézier curve.

Example:

```
<!DOCTYPE html>
<html>
<body>

<p> Using methods: quadraticCurveTo() </p>
<canvas id="myCanvas" width="300" height="350"
style="border:1px solid #d3d3d3;">

Your browser doesn't support the HTML5 canvas
tag.</canvas>

<script>
var cnv = document.getElementById("my_Canvas");
var ctx = cnv.getContext("2d");
ctx.beginPath();
ctx.moveTo(20, 20);
ctx.quadraticCurveTo(20, 120, 200, 120);
ctx.stroke();

    </script>
</body>
</html>
```

- bezierCurveTo(): It creates a cubic Bézier curve.

Example:

```
<!DOCTYPE html>
<html>
<body>
```

```
<p> Using methods: quadraticCurveTo() </p>
<canvas id="myCanvas" width="300" height="350"
style="border:1px solid #d3d3d3;">

Your browser doesn't support the HTML5 canvas
tag.</canvas>

<script>
var cnv = document.getElementById("my_Canvas");
var ctx = cnv.getContext("2d");
ctx.beginPath();
ctx.moveTo(19, 19);
ctx.bezierCurveTo(10, 101, 201, 101, 201, 20);
ctx.stroke();
</script>
</body>
</html>
```

- arc(): It creates an arc/curve (used to create circles or parts of circles).

Example:

```
<!DOCTYPE html>
<html>
<body>

<p> Using methods: arc() </p>
<canvas id="myCanvas" width="300" height="350"
style="border:1px solid #d3d3d3;">

Your browser doesn't support the HTML5 canvas
tag.</canvas>

<script>
var cnv = document.getElementById("my_Canvas");
var ctx = cnv.getContext("2d");
ctx.beginPath();
ctx.arc(100, 175, 80, 0, 2 * Math.PI);
ctx.stroke();
</script>
</body>
</html>
```

- arcTo(): It creates an arc/curve between two tangents.

Example:

```
<!DOCTYPE html>
<html>
<body>

<p> Using methods: arcTo() </p>
<canvas id="my_Canvas" width="300" height="350"
style="border:1px solid #d3d3d3;">

Your browser doesn't support the HTML5 canvas
tag.</canvas>

<script>
var cnv = document.getElementById("m_yCanvas");
var ctx = cnv.getContext("2d");
ctx.beginPath();
ctx.moveTo(20, 20);                   // Create a
starting point
ctx.lineTo(100, 20);                  // Create a
horizontal line
ctx.arcTo(150, 20, 150, 170, 50);  // Create an
arc
ctx.lineTo(150, 120);                 // Continue
with vertical line
ctx.stroke();
</script>
</body>
</html>
```

- isPointInPath(): It returns true if the specified point is in the current path, otherwise false.

Example:

```
<!DOCTYPE html>
<html>
<body>

<p> Using methods: isPointInPath() </p>
<canvas id="my_Canvas" width="300" height="350"
style="border:1px solid #d3d3d3;">
```

```
Your browser doesn't support the HTML5 canvas
tag.</canvas>

<script>
var cnv = document.getElementById("my_Canvas");
var ctx = cnv.getContext("2d");
ctx.rect(20, 20, 150, 100);
if (ctx.isPointInPath(20, 50)) {
  ctx.stroke();
};
</script>
</body>
</html>
```

You can use the following methods to style transforms:

- scale(): It scales the current drawing larger or smaller.

- rotate(): It rotates the current drawing.

- translate(): It remaps the (0,0) position on the canvas.

- transform(): It replaces the current transformation matrix for the drawing.

- setTransform(): It resets the current transform to the identity matrix. It then runs transform().

You can use the following methods to style text:

- font: It sets or returns the current font properties for the text content.

- textAlign: It sets or returns the current alignment of the text content.

- textBaseline: It sets or returns the current text baseline used when drawing text.

- fillText(): It draws "filled" text on the canvas.

- strokeText(): It draws text on the canvas (no padding).

- measureText(): It returns an object that contains the width of the specified text.

To stylize an image drawing, you can use the following methods:

- drawImage(): It draws an image, canvas, and video onto the canvas.

You can use the following methods to style a pixel:

- width: It returns the width of the ImageData object.
- height: It returns the height of the ImageData object.
- data: It returns an object that contains the image data of the specified ImageData object.
- createImageData(): It creates a new empty ImageData object.
- getImageData(): It returns an ImageData object that copies the pixel data for the specified rectangle to the canvas.
- putImageData(): It puts the image data (from the specified ImageData object) back onto the canvas.

You can use the following methods for folding:

- globalAlpha sets or returns the current drawing alpha or transparency value.
- globalCompositeOperation sets or returns a method for rendering a new image over an existing image.
- save() saves the state of the current context.
- restore() returns the previously saved path state and attributes.
- createEvent().
- getContext().
- toDataURL().

Rendering Context

The <canvas> element creates a fixed-size canvas that exposes one or more rendering contexts that are used to create and manipulate displayed content.[18] In this section, we will focus on the context of 2D rendering. Other contexts might provide different types of rendering. For example, WebGL uses a 3D context based on OpenGL ES.

Initially, the canvas is blank. To display something, a script must access and draw from the rendering context. The <canvas> element has one method called getContext() that is used to get the rendering context and its drawing functions. getContext() takes one parameter, the context type.

```
var c = document.getElementById("myCanvas");
var ctx = c.getContext("2d");
```

The line in the script retrieves the node in the DOM representing the <canvas> element by calling the document.getElementById() method. Once you have an element node, you can access the drawing context using its getContext() method.

Example:

```
<!DOCTYPE html>
  <head>
    <title>Page Title</title>
    <script>
     function draw() {
        const canvas = document.
getElementById("tutorial");
        if (canvas.getContext) {
           const ctx = canvas.getContext("2d");
        }
     }
    </script>
    <style>
      canvas {
        border: 1px solid black;
      }
    </style>
</head>
<body onload="draw();">
   <h1> Make a circle </h1>
   <canvas id="tutorial" width="150"
height="150"></canvas>

</body>
</html
```

The script contains a function called draw() that runs when the page has finished loading. The listening to the load event on the document. The function can also be called setTimeout(), setInterval(), or any other event handler if the page was loaded first.

Drawing Shapes with Canvas

We can get into the detail of how to draw shapes on the canvas. You will learn how to draw rectangles, triangles, lines, arcs, and curves and will be introduced to some basic shapes. Working with paths is needed when drawing objects on the canvas, and we'll see how this can be done with the help of some examples.

Using attributes on the canvas:

- height: The height of the coordinate space in CSS pixels. The default value is 150.

- moz-opaque: If the canvas knows it's not translucent, painting performance can be optimized. Only Mozilla-based browsers support this; use the standardized canvas.getContext('2d', { alpha: false }) instead.

- width: Width of the coordinate space in CSS pixels. The default value is 300.

Canvas Coordinates

The HTML canvas is a two-dimensional grid. The upper left corner of the canvas has the coordinates (0,0).

Now mouse over the rectangle below to see its x and y coordinates:

```
<!DOCTYPE html>
 <head>
   <title>Page Title</title>
   <style>
body {
  margin: 0;
  padding: 30px;
  font-family: sans-serif;
  font-size: 14px;
}
```

```css
.holder {
  display: inline-block;
  position: relative;
  text-align: center;
}

h2 {
  position: absolute;
  width: 80%;
  top: 50%;
  left: 50%;
  transform: translate(-50%,-50%);
  color: #fff;
  pointer-events: none;
}

span {
  display: block;
}

canvas {
  display: block;
  width: 600px;
  height: 300px;
  background-color: #AB47BC;
}

ol, ul {
  line-height: 1.3;
  max-width: 500px;
}

li {
  padding-bottom:. 7em;
}

</style>
  </head>
<body>
  <div class="holder">
    <h2> x,y  coordinates (as per canvas):<span
id="x">x: 0</span><span id="y">y: 0</span></h2>
```

```
    <canvas></canvas>
  </div>


<script>

var canvas = document.querySelector('canvas'),
  ctx = canvas.getContext('2d'),
  cw = ctx.canvas.width,
  ch = ctx.canvas.height,
  receiveX = document.getElementById('x'),
  receiveY = document.getElementById('y');

function normalizeCanvasCoords (x, y) {
  var boundingBox = canvas.getBoundingClientRect();
  return {
    x: (x - boundingBox.left) * (cw / boundingBox.
width),
    y: (y - boundingBox.top) * (ch / boundingBox.
height)
  }
}

function updateText (x, y) {
  var coordX = 'x: ' + Math.floor(x),
    coordY = 'y: ' + Math.floor(y);
  receiveX.innerHTML = coordX;
  receiveY.innerHTML = coordY;
}

canvas.onmousemove = function (e) {
  var mouseX = e.clientX,
    mouseY = e.clientY,
    location = normalizeCanvasCoords(mouseX, mouseY);
  updateText(location.x, location.y)
}

</script>
</body>
</html
```

HTML Canvas x, y coordinates (as per canvas).

To draw a long, straight line on a canvas, you can use the following methods:

- moveTo(x,y) – It defines the starting point of the line.

- lineTo(x,y) – It defines the ending point of the line.

Example:

```
<!DOCTYPE html>
  <head>
    <title>Page Title</title>
    <style>
</style>
  </head>
<body>
  <div class="holder">
    <h1> Draw a Line </h1>
    <canvas id="myCanvas" width="150"
height="150"></canvas>
  </div>
<script>

var canvas = document.getElementById("myCanvas");
var ctx = canvas.getContext("2d");
ctx.moveTo(0, 0);
ctx.lineTo(200, 100);
ctx.stroke();

</script>
</body>
</html
```

Draw a Line

Draw a line using HTML canvas.

Draw a Circle

To draw a circle on the canvas, use the following methods:[19]

- beginPath() – Begins the path.

- arc(x,y,r,star-tangle,end-angle) – Creates an arc/curve. To create a circle using arc(): Set the start angle to 0 and the end angle to 2*Math.PI. The x and y parameters define the x and y coordinates of the center of the circle. The parameter r defines the radius of the circle.

```
<!DOCTYPE html>
 <head>
   <title>Page Title</title>
   <style>
</style>
  </head>
<body>
  <div class="holder">
    <h1> Draw a Circle </h1>
    <canvas id="myCanvas" width="150" height="150">
</canvas>
  </div>

  <script>
    var canvas = document.getElementById("myCanvas");
    var ctx = canvas.getContext("2d");
    ctx.beginPath();
    ctx.arc(95,50,40,0,2*Math.PI);
    ctx.stroke();
    </script>

</body>
</html
```

HTML Canvas Gradients

Gradients can use to fill rectangles, circles, lines, text, etc. The shapes on the canvas are not limited to solid colors. There are two different types of gradients:

- createLinearGradient(x,y,x1,y1) – It creates a linear gradient.

- createRadialGradient(x,y,r,x1,y1,r1It) – It creates a radial/circular gradient.

The canvas_variable.createLinearGradient() method of the Canvas 2D API creates a gradient along the line connecting the two given coordinates. This method returns a linear CanvasGradient. If you want to apply to a shape, the gradient must be assigned to the fillStyle or strokeStyle properties.

Here is the syntax, createLinearGradient(x0, y0, x1, y1)

Parameters:

- x0 – The x-axis coordinates the starting point.

- y0 – The y-axis coordinates the starting point.

- x1 – The x-axis coordinate of the end point.

- y1 – The y-axis coordinate of the end point.

Example:

```
<!DOCTYPE html>
 <head>
   <title>Page Title</title>
   <style>
</style>
   </head>
<body>
  <div class="holder">
    <h1> Draw a Reactangle (with a method
addColorStop ) </h1>
    <canvas id="myCanvas" width="150"
height="150"></canvas>
  </div>
```

```
  <script>
 var c = document.getElementById("myCanvas");
var ctx = c.getContext("2d");

// It creates gradient
var grd = ctx.createLinearGradient(0, 0, 201, 0);
grd.addColorStop(0, "blue");

// Fill with gradient
ctx.fillStyle = grd;
ctx.fillRect(10, 10, 150, 80);
    </script>

</body>
</html>
```

Another example of gradient:

```
<!DOCTYPE html>
 <head>
   <title>Page Title</title>
   <style>
</style>
  </head>
<body>
  <div class="holder">
    <h1> Draw a Reactangle (with two method
addColorStop )
</h1>
    <canvas id="my_Canvas" width="150"
height="150">
</canvas>
  </div>

  <script>
 var cnv = document.getElementById("my_Canvas");
var ctx = cnv.getContext("2d");

// Create gradient
var grd = ctx.createLinearGradient(0, 0, 201, 0);
grd.addColorStop(0, "blue");
grd.addColorStop(1, "red");
```

```
// Fill with gradient
ctx.fillStyle = grd;
ctx.fillRect(10, 10, 150, 80);
    </script>

</body>
</html
```

Benefits of Using Canvas[20]

- Animation – Every object can be created on the canvas and also the object can be animated. It allows developers to create all levels of animation.

- Flexible – It can help draw any shape, picture, or structure like polygons, shaping, activities, and even games. It is also possible to add video and audio.

- Interactivity – Canvas is fully interactive and can respond to user actions by listening to keyboard, mouse, or touch. So the developer is not limited to just static graphics and images.

- Popularity – Canvas has become popular very quickly and steadily due to its widely useful features.

- Browser/Platform support – All major browsers are supported and can be obtained on a wide range of devices including desktops, tablets, and smartphones.

- Effectively run ads – Many web developers still use third-party tools like Adobe Flash to run ads and banners on websites. These third-party tools often increase load times. Developers can use the HTML5 canvas element to run ads and banners on a web page without using any third-party tools or extensions. It allows developers to run ads and banners on a web page without affecting loading speed and user experience.

- Support latest browser – Currently, the HTML5 canvas element is supported by the latest versions of widely used web browsers such as Chrome, Firefox, Safari, and Opera. It allows users to access 2D graphics developed using the canvas element on major web browsers. The improved compatibility further helps web developers effectively use the HTML5 element to dynamically draw various 2D graphics on web pages.

- Simplify 2D drawing operations – Web developers often have to write longer lines of code to dynamically render 2D graphics. Some developers even use specific libraries and plugins to speed up 2D drawing operations. It also allows programmers to draw various 2D graphics on web pages using JavaScript. Developers can use the HTML element to draw 2D graphics without writing additional code, keeping the web application source code clean and maintainable.

- Create simple and complex animations – In addition to simplifying 2D drawing operations, canvas elements allow programmers to animate various objects. Web developers can use the HTML5 element to create both simple as well as complex animations on a web page. They can use custom JavaScript code to display different levels of animations running on a web page.

Drawing Text on Canvas

If you want to draw text on the HTML canvas, we need to start by defining what this font should look like. For this, we use ctx.font, which has the same syntax as the CSS font property. For example, if we wanted our font to be Arial 88px bold, we could define our font as:

```
let canvas = document.getElementById('canvas');
let ctx = canvas.getContext('2d');
ctx.font = 'bold 88px Arial';
```

This string gives us the base style of our font, but if we want to change the color, we can use the fillStyle property again (which works the same as for shapes). Let's make our font white:

```
ctx.fillStyle = 'white'
```

To draw text on a canvas, the important properties and methods are:

- font – it defines the font properties for the text.
- fillText(text,x,y) – it draws "filled" text on the canvas.
- strokeText(text,x,y) –it draws text on the canvas (no fill).

CHAPTER SUMMARY

In this chapter, we studied HTML game development with some methods of 2D and 3D animations. We also discussed canvas in HTML.

NOTES

1. HTML Introduction for Gaming – https://gamedevacademy.org/how-to-make-a-html5-game/#What_exactly_is_an_HTML5_game, accessed on September 14, 2022.
2. HTML Building Blocks – https://www.schudio.com/understanding-html-and-the-building-blocks-that-come-with-it/#:~:text=To%20fully%20understand%20the%20basics,%3B%20tags%2C%20elements%20and%20attributes, accessed on September 14, 2022.
3. HTML5 Game Fundamentals – https://www.envato.com/blog/building-your-first-html5-game/, accessed on September 14, 2022.
4. Goals – https://www.envato.com/blog/building-your-first-html5-game/, accessed on September 14, 2022.
5. User Interacting – https://www.envato.com/blog/building-your-first-html5-game/, accessed on September 14, 2022.
6. HTML5 Framework – http://techslides.com/html5-game-engines-and-frameworks, accessed on September 14, 2022.
7. HTML5 Game Development Benefits – https://hacks.mozilla.org/2013/09/getting-started-with-html5-game-development/, accessed on September 14, 2022.
8. Benefits – https://js13kgames.com/p/top10-advantages.html, accessed on September 14, 2022.
9. Facts – https://www.juegostudio.com/blog/things-you-didnt-know-about-html5-game-development#:~:text=HTML5%20Game%20Development%20Uses%20WebGL,the%20library%2C%20ready%20for%20use, accessed on September 14, 2022.
10. HTML Facts – https://www.juegostudio.com/blog/things-you-didnt-know-about-html5-game-development#:~:text=HTML5%20Game%20Development%20Uses%20WebGL,the%20library%2C%20ready%20for%20use, accessed on September 14, 2022.
11. Features – https://www.uniassignment.com/essay-samples/information-technology/principles-for-game-development-in-html5-information-technology-essay.php, accessed on September 14, 2022.
12. Canvas Graphics in HTML – https://developer.mozilla.org/en-US/docs/Web/API/Canvas_API/Tutorial, accessed on September 14, 2022.
13. HTML Canvas – https://www.geeksforgeeks.org/html-canvas-basics/, accessed on September 15, 2022.
14. HTML Canvas – https://developer.mozilla.org/en-US/docs/Web/API/Canvas_API/Tutorial/Basic_usage, accessed on September 15, 2022.
15. Canvas Class – https://www.dofactory.com/html/canvas/class, accessed on September 15, 2022.

16. Canvas Methods – https://www.w3schools.com/tags/ref_canvas.asp, accessed on September 15, 2022.

17. Canvas Property – http://drawingincode.com/lessons/reference/fill_style/index.html, accessed on September 16, 2022.

18. Canvas Benefits – https://www.tutorialscampus.com/html5/canvas.htm, accessed on September 15, 2022.

19. HTML Canvas Circle – https://www.w3schools.com/graphics/canvas_gradients.asp, accessed on September 15, 2022.

20. Canvas Benefits – http://www.allaboutweb.biz/html5-canvas/, accessed on September 15, 2022.

Cheat Sheet

HTML is basically the building block of all web pages.[1] It provides proper structure to the content appearing on a web page, such as images, text, and videos, by creating a basic skeleton. It is still so useful today, the reason being that no matter what framework or language we use to develop a website, the output will be rendered in HTML.

HTML elements are basically the building blocks of HTML pages. You can use HTML constructs to insert other objects such as images and interactive forms into the rendered page. HTML provides a method to create structured documents by marking up the structural semantics of text, such as text formatting, headings, paragraphs, lists, links, quotes, and other elements. HTML elements are delimited by tags written in curly braces. Tags such as and place content directly on the page. Other tags, such as, provide information about the body of the document and can contain other tags as subelements. Browsers do not display HTML tags themselves but use them to interpret page content.

Hypertext is text displayed on a system or other electronic device that contains links to other text that the user can get immediate access, usually by clicking a mouse or pressing a key. In addition to text, hypertext can include tables, lists, forms, images, and other presentation elements. It is an easy-to-use and flexible format for exchanging information over the Internet. The markup uses a series of markup tags to characterize text elements in a document and tell the web browser what the document should look like.

HTML can embed programs written in various scripting languages, such as JavaScript, to affect the behavior and content of web pages. CSS embedding defines the appearance and layout of content. The W3C, the

DOI: 10.1201/9781003357537-5

former maintainer of HTML and now the maintainer of CSS standards, has supported the use of CSS in explicit presentation of HTML since 1997.

POPULARITY

When Tim Berners-Lee came up with the design to allow easy document sharing at CERN in 1980. The most current and widely used version of HTML is HTML5. The W3C is the community responsible for developing open standards to ensure the long-term growth of the Web. When browser vendors adopt these standards they become standards and browsers such as Chrome, Firefox, and Safari implement them.

HTML is widely used and accepted as it is easy to learn and write because it is human readable. The ease of learning and developing HTML websites makes it very popular.

HTML CHEAT SHEET

Beginning web developers sometimes need a simple and quick reference list of basic HTML tags, codes, and attributes, and that's when the HTML Cheat Sheet comes in handy.[2] The only purpose of this Cheat Sheet is to provide you with some quick and accurate ready-made code snippets and the necessary HTML tags and attributes to help you with your website.

The list of topics we will discuss is given below in categories in which they use:

- Heading Tags
- Container Tags
- Document Section
- Sectioning Tags
- Text Formatting Tags
- List Tags
- Table Tags
- Form Tags
- Multimedia Tags
- Characters and Symbols
- Attributes

HTML DOCUMENT SUMMARY

Main Root: The <html> represents the root (top-level element) of the HTML document, which is also called the document element because it defines the entire HTML document. It has a start <html> tag and an end </html> tag.

<html>

This tag specifies that the web page is written in HTML. It appears on the first and last line website. It is mainly used to display that the site uses HTML5 – the latest version of language. It is also known as the root element; tag can be considered a parent tag for every other tag used on the page.

Syntax:

```
<html> ... </html>
```

Example:

```
<!DOCTYPE html>
<html>
  <head>
    <title> HTML </title>
  </head>

  <body>
  </body>

</html>
```

<head>

This tag is used to define metadata about web page. It contains the name of the website, its dependencies (JS and CSS scripts), font usage, etc.

Syntax:

```
<head> ... </head>
```

Example:

```
<!DOCTYPE html>
<html>
  <head>
    <title> HTML </title>
  </head>
```

```
  <body>
  </body>

</html>
```

<title>

As the name suggests, the tag contains the website name and title. You can see it in the header of your browser for every web page you open in the browser. The search engines use this tag to extract the theme of the website, which is quite convenient in evaluating relevant search results.

Syntax:

```
<title> ... </title>
```

Example:

```
<!DOCTYPE html>
<html>
  <head>
    <title> HTML </title>
  </head>

  <body>
  </body>

</html>
```

<body>

Everything a user can see on a web page is written inside this tag. It is a container for all contents website. There can be a single <body> element in a document.

Syntax:

```
<body> ... </body>
```

Example:

```
<!DOCTYPE html>
<html>
  <head>
    <title> HTML </title>
  </head>
```

```
  <body>
  </body>

</html>
```

HTML DOCUMENT INFORMATION

<base>

It is used to determine the base URL of your website, this tag creates links to internal links on your site cleaner.

Syntax:

```
<base/>
```

Example:

```
<!DOCTYPE html>
<html>
  <head>
    <base href="https://www.google.com/"
target="_blank">
  </head>

  <body>
  </body>

</html>
```

<meta>

This is the metadata tag for the web page. It may be useful to mention the author of the page, keywords, original publication date, etc.

Syntax:

```
<meta/>
```

Example:

```
<!DOCTYPE html>
<html>
  <head>
    <meta charset="UTF-8">
    <meta name="description" content="Free Web
tutorials">
```

```
    <meta name="keywords" content="HTML, CSS,
JavaScript">
    <meta name="author" content="John Doe">
    <meta content="width=device-width, initial-
scale=1.0" name="viewport" >
  </head>

  <body>
  </body>

</html>
```

\<link>

It is used to link to external scripts web page. Usually, it is used for inclusion styles. The \<link> tag is often used to link to external (outside) stylesheets on your website.

Syntax:

```
<link>
```

Example:

```
<!DOCTYPE html>
<html>
  <head>
    <link rel="stylesheet" href="styles.css">
  </head>

  <body>
  </body>

</html>
```

\<style>

A style tag can be used as an alternative to an external stylesheet or supplement it. It contains information about the appearance of the website.

Syntax:

```
<style> … </style>
```

Example:

```
<!DOCTYPE html>
<html>
  <head>
    <style>
  h1 {
        color: red;
}
  p {
        color: blue;
  }
    </style>
  </head>

  <body>
  </body>
  <h1>
    Lorem ipsum dolor oo sit amet, consectetur
adipiscing elit.</h1>
    <p> Aenean finibus lectus vel nibh porttitor
efficitur eu eget diam.</p>
</html>
```

<script>

It is used to add code snippets, usually in JavaScript, to make the website dynamic. It can also be used for this; a link to an external script is sufficient.

Syntax:

```
<script> … </script>
```

Example:

```
<!DOCTYPE html>
<html>
  <head>
    <style>

  p {
    color: blue;
```

```
font-size: 20px;
}
  </style>
</head>

<body>

<p id="demo"> </p>

<script>
document.getElementById("demo").innerHTML = " You
are learning HTML !";
</script>
</body>
</html>
```

HTML DOCUMENT STRUCTURE TAGS

`<h1 to h6>`

There are six different variants of writing the headline. `<h1>` tag has the largest font size, while `<h6>` has the smallest.

Syntax:

```
<h1 to h6> … </h1 to h6>
```

Example:

```
<!DOCTYPE html>
<html>
  <head>
    <style>
  h1 {color: light blue;}
  h2 {color: lightcoral;}
  h3 {color: light cyan;}
  h4 {color: lightgray;}
  h5 {color: light pink;}
  h6 {color: light salmon;}

    </style>
  </head>

  <body>
  </body>
```

```
<h1> Lorem ipsum dolor oo sit amet, consectetur
adipiscing elit.</h1>
    <h2>  Aenean finibus lectus vel nibh porttitor
efficitur eu eget diam. </h2>
     <h3> Integer in leo quis turpis sollicitudin
accumsan. </h3>
     <h4> Ut viverra magna quis blandit porttitor.
</h4>
<h5> Morbi ornare odio sit amet quam mattis
auctor. </h5>
<h6> Nam ac orci eu tellus venenatis accumsan.
</h6>
</html>
```

<div>

The content of a website is usually divided into blocks, specified by the div tag.

Syntax:

```
<div> … </div>
```

Example:

```
<!DOCTYPE html>
<html>
  <head>
    <style>
div {
border:1px solid black;
padding:10px
}

    </style>
  </head>
  <body>

  <div>
    Duis ultricies tempor ligula, eu tempus ligula
pellentesque sit amet.
    In nibh est, finibus scelerisque tortor
porttitor, consequat condimentum dolor.
```

```
     Aliquam eu nulla purus. Cras risus sem,
vestibulum in auctor eget, placerat in turpis. Ut
consequat, odio vel euismod sagittis, ex sem
convallis erat, non gravida massa turpis in elit.
Nullam nisl odio, semper quis turpis mollis,
     euismod interdum sapien. Nulla vulputate
ligula a mollis consectetur.
   </div>
   <div>
     Duis ultricies tempor ligula, eu tempus ligula
pellentesque sit amet.
     In nibh est, finibus scelerisque tortor
porttitor, consequat condimentum dolor.
      Aliquam eu nulla purus. Cras risus sem,
vestibulum in auctor eget, placerat in turpis. Ut
consequat, odio vel euismod sagittis, ex sem
convallis erat, non gravida massa turpis in elit.
Nullam nisl odio, semper quis turpis mollis,
     euismod interdum sapien. Nulla vulputate
ligula a mollis consectetur.
   </div>
   <div>
     Duis ultricies tempor ligula, eu tempus ligula
pellentesque sit amet.
     In nibh est, finibus scelerisque tortor
porttitor, consequat condimentum dolor.
      Aliquam eu nulla purus. Cras risus sem,
vestibulum in auctor eget, placerat in turpis. Ut
consequat, odio vel euismod sagittis, ex sem
convallis erat, non gravida massa turpis in elit.
Nullam nisl odio, semper quis turpis mollis,
     euismod interdum sapien. Nulla vulputate
ligula a mollis consectetur.
   </div>
</html>
```

<span>

This tag embeds inline elements such as an image, icon, or emoticon without destroying formatting page styling.

Syntax:

```
<span> … </span>
```

Example:

```
<!DOCTYPE html>
<html>
<head>
<title> HTML </title>
</head>
<body>
   <p> This book is about <span style="color:blue;
font-size: 50px; background-color: yellow;"> HTML
</span>  and you are learning it.</p>
</body>
</html>
```

`<p>`

It is just a plain text that is placed inside this tag.

Syntax:

```
<p> ... </p>
```

Example:

```
<!DOCTYPE html>
<html>
<head>
<title> HTML </title>
</head>
<body>
   <p> This book is about HTML and you are learning
it.</p>
</body>
</html>
```

`<br>`

It is a line break for web pages. It is used when you want to write a new line.

Syntax:

```
<br/>
```

Example:

```
<!DOCTYPE html>
<html>
<head>
<title> HTML </title>
</head>
<body>
  <p> This book is about HTML </p> <br/>
  <p> You are learning it. </p>
</body>
</html>
```

<hr>

It is similar to the above tag. But besides that switching to the next line also draws that marker a horizontal bar indicating the end partition.

Syntax:

```
<hr/>
```

Example:

```
<!DOCTYPE html>
<html>
<head>
<title> HTML </title>
</head>
<body>
  <p> This book is about HTML </p> <hr/>
  <p> You are learning it. </p>
</body>
</html>
```

TEXT FORMATTING AND INLINE TEXT SEMANTICS

Text formatting is used in HTML to make a document look more complex and attractive. HTML inline text semantics are used to define the meaning, structure, or style of a word, line, or arbitrary text.

<strong>

It indicates text bold and is used to emphasize a point. Typically, browsers render their content in bold.

Syntax:

```
<strong> ... </strong>
```

Example:

```
<!DOCTYPE html>
<head>
<title> HTML </title>
</head>
<body>
  <p> <strong> Warning </strong>: Shake well
before use! </p>
</body>
</html>
```

`<b>`

Alternative to the above tag, it also creates bold text and makes the text enclosed within these tags bold.

Syntax:

```
<b> ... </b>
```

Example:

```
<!DOCTYPE html>
<head>
<title> HTML </title>
</head>
<body>
  <p> <b> Warning </b>: Shake well before use!
</p>
</body>
</html>
```

`<em>`

Another emphasis tag, but this displays text in italics. It can be nested as well, where each level of nesting indicates a greater degree of emphasis.

Syntax:

```
<em> ... </em>
```

Example:

```
<!DOCTYPE html>
<head>
<title> HTML </title>
</head>
<body>
  <p> <em> Warning </em>: Shake well before use!
</p>
</body>
</html>
```

<i>

Also used to display text in italics, but does not emphasize it like the above tag.

Syntax:

```
<i> … </i>
```

Example:

```
<!DOCTYPE html>
<head>
<title> HTML </title>
</head>
<body>
  <p> <i> Warning </i>: Shake well before use!
</p>
</body>
</html>
```

<tt>

It is used for formatting typewriter-like text. But it is no longer supported in HTML5.

Syntax:

```
<tt> … </tt>
```

<strike>

Another old tag, it is used to draw a line at the center of the text, so as to make it appear deleted or no longer useful. But it is no longer supported in HTML5.

Syntax:

```
<strike> ... </strike>
```

<cite>

This tag is for describing the title of a creative work (e.g. book, paper, essay, poem, song, painting, etc.).

Syntax:

```
<cite> ... </cite>
```

Example:

```
<!DOCTYPE html>
<head>
<title> HTML </title>
</head>
<body>
   <img src="https://images.pexels.com/
photos/1591061/pexels-photo-1591061.jpeg?auto=comp
ress&cs=tinysrgb&w=400" width="220" height="277"
alt="The Scream">
   <p> <cite> HTML: </cite> Hyper Text Markup
Language </p> </body>
</html>
```

<del> ... </del>

It denotes text that has been deleted from a document. Usually strike a line through deleted text.

<ins> ... </ins>

It denotes text that has been inserted into the web page. It usually underlines inserted text.

<blockquote> ... </blockquote>

The quotation often writes into this tag. It is used with the <cite> tag.

<q> ... </q>

It is similar to the above tag but for shorter quotations.

<abbr> ... </abbr>

It denotes abbreviations, along with the full forms. An abbreviation like "HTML", "CSS", "Mr.", "Dr.".

<address> ... </address>

It denotes the contact information for any user of a blog or site. The information can be an email address, residential address, phone number, social media account, etc. It usually renders in italics.

<dfn> ... </dfn>

It specifies a term that is to be defined within the content. The <dfn> tag must contain the definition/explanation for the term.

<code> ... </code>

This is used to display a piece of computer code and code snippets within a paragraph.

<samp> ... </smap>

Defines sample output from a computer program. The default font is monospace.

<kbd> ... </kbd>

It is used to define keyboard input. The default font is monospace.

<var> ... </var>

It defines a variable in programming or in a mathematical expression. The default font is italics.

<pre> ... </pre>

It is displayed in a fixed-width font and the text preserves both spaces and line breaks. The text will be shown exactly as written in the HTML source code.

_{...}

Used for writing a subscript. It appears half a character below the normal line and is sometimes rendered in a smaller font.

^{...}

The <sup> tag defines superscript text. Its text appears half a character above the normal line, sometimes rendered in a smaller font. It can be used for footnotes in MS Word.

<small> ... </small>

It reduces text size. It often refers to redundant or invalid information.

HTML LINKS

A link or hyperlink is a basically connection from one web resource to another. Its links allow users to move from one page to another on any server.

SETTING TARGETS FOR LINKS

The target attribute tells the web browser where to open the linked document. There are four defined targets and each target name begins with an underscore character (_):

- _blank – It opens the document in a new window or tab.

- _parent – It opens the document in the parent window.

- _self – It opens the document in the same window or tab as the source document. This is the default value, so it is not necessary to specify this value explicitly.

- _top – It opens the document in a full browser window.

<a href=""> ... </a>

It is an anchor tag. Primarily used for including hyperlinks.

<a href=" mailto: "> ... </a>

This anchor tag attributes with value "mailto" dedicated to sending emails.

<a href="tel://###-###"> ... </a>

This anchor tag attributes with value "tel" mentioning contact numbers. As the numbers are clickable, this can be beneficial for mobile users.

<a href="tel://###-###"> ... </a>

This anchor tag attributes with value "tel" mentioning contact numbers. As the numbers are clickable, this can be beneficial for phone users.

<a name="name"> ... </a>

This anchor tag attributes with value "name" can be used to quickly navigate to a different part of the web page.

<a href="#name"> ... </a>

A variation of the above tag, only meant to navigate to a div section of the web page.

HTML LISTS

Lists can be either numeric, alphabetical, bulleted, or other symbols. For a simple document, you can specify the list type and list items in HTML. There are three types of lists in HTML:

- Unordered List: It is used to group a set of items in no particular order.

- Sorted List: It is used to group a set of items in a specific order.

- Description List: It is used to display name/value pairs such as terms and definitions.

Here are various tags used in list.

<ol>

The tag for ordered or numbered list of items. It is rendered as a numbered list.

Syntax:

```
<ol> … </ol>
```

<ul>

It is contrary to the above tag and is used for the unordered list of items. It is rendered as a bulleted list.

Syntax:

```
<ul> … </ul>
```

\<li\>

It represents individual item as part of a list.

Syntax:

```
<li> ... </li>
```

\<dl\>

Tag for a list of items with definitions and also for a description list. It encloses a list of groups of terms (it is specified using the \<dt\> element) and descriptions.

Syntax:

```
<li> ... </li>
```

\<dt\>

The definition of a term inline with body content and used in conjunction with \<dl\> to specify a term in a description or definition list.

Syntax:

```
<dt> ... </dt>
```

\<dd\>

The description for the defined term used in conjunction with \<dl\> to describe a term/name in a description list.

Syntax:

```
<dd> ... </dd>
```

HTML FORMS

\<form\> ... \</form\>

The parent tag for a form action="URL" the URL here is where the form data will be submitted once the user fills it and represents a document section containing interactive controls for submitting information.

Here are some attributes of the form tag:

- method="": It specifies that the HTTP method (POST or GET) would be used to submit the form.

- enctype="": The only for the POST method, this dictates the data encoding scheme to be used when the form is submitted.

- Autocomplete: It determines if the form has autocomplete enabled.

- Novalidate: It determines whether the form should be validated before submission.

- accept-charsets: It determines character encodings when form is submitted.

- Target: After submission, the response is displayed wherever this refers to, usually having the following values: _blank, _self, _parent, and _top.

<input>

The HTML <input> is used to create interactive controls for web-based forms in order to take input from the user. Input type is determined by alphabets, number, color, file, and so on of attributes.

Here are some attributes of the form tag:

- type="": It specifies what type of input (text, data, and password) is required from the user.

- name="": It specifies the name of the input field.

- value="": It specifies the currently contained value input field.

- size = "": It specifies the width of the input element (number of characters).

- maxlength="": It specifies the maximum number of characters allowed in the input field.

- Required: It enters mandatory filling of the input field user. If required, the form cannot be submitted the field will remain blank.

- width = "": It specifies the width of the input element, in pixel values.

- height = "": It specifies the height of the input element, in pixel values.

- wildcard ="": It can be used to give the user advice about the nature of required data.

- pattern="": It specifies the regular expression that can be used to look for patterns in the user's text.

- min="": The min value allowed for an <input> element.

- max="": The max value allowed for the <input> element.

- Autofocus: It forces to focus on an input element on a web page that will load completely.

- Forbidden: It disables the input element. The user can no longer enter the dates.

<label>…</label>

This tag is used to specify a label or title for the form's <input> element. The <label> element is useful for screen reader users because the screen reader reads the label aloud when the user focuses on the input element. It also helps users who have trouble clicking on small options (like radio buttons or checkboxes). The "for attribute" of the <label> tag should match with the "id attribute" of the <input> element to join them together.

Example:

```
<!DOCTYPE html>
<html>
<head>
<body>
  <form action="index.php">
    <input type="radio" id="HTML" name="language"
value="HTML">
    <label for="HTML"> HTML </label> <br>
    <input type="radio" id="CSS" name="language"
value="CSS">
    <label for="CSS"> CSS </label> <br>
    <input type="radio" id="javascript"
name="language" value="JavaScript">
    <label for="javascript"> JavaScript </label>
<br> <br>
    <input type="submit" value="Submit">
  </form>
</body>
  </html>
```

It works with several elements such as:

- <input type="checkbox">

- <input type="color">

- <input type="date">
- <input type="DateTime-local">
- <input type="email">
- <input type="file">
- <input type="month">
- <input type="number">
- <input type="password">
- <input type="radio">
- <input type="range">
- <input type="search">
- <input type="tel">
- <input type="text">
- <input type="time">
- <input type="URL">
- <input type="week">
- <meter>
- <progress>
- <select>
- <textarea>

<textarea>

The <textarea> element is used to create a multi-line plain-text editing control, often used in a form, to collect user inputs like comments or reviews, and represents a control that provides a menu of options to select from.

Syntax:

```
<textarea>...</textarea>
```

Example:

```
<!DOCTYPE html>
<html>
<head>
  <style>
    body {background: #F0F0F0;}

h2 {margin-left: 55px;}

textarea {
  margin-top: 10px;
  margin-left: 50px;
  width: 600px;
  height: 200px;
  background: none repeat scroll 0 0 rgba(0, 0, 0,
0.07);
  border-image: none;
  border-radius: 6px 6px 6px 6px;
  border-style: none solid solid none;
  border-width: medium 1px 1px medium;
  box-shadow: 0 1px 2px rgba(0, 0, 0, 0.12) inset;
  color: #555555;
  font-family: "Helvetica
Neue",Helvetica,Arial,sans-serif;
  font-size: 1em;
  line-height: 1.4em;
  padding: 5px 8px;
  transition: background-color 0.2s ease 0s;
}

textarea:focus {
    background: none repeat scroll 0 0 #FFFFFF;
    outline-width: 0;
}
  </style>
<body>
  <h2> Textarea </h2>

<textarea placeholder="This is an awesome comment
box" rows="20" name="comment[text]" id="comment_
text" cols="40" class="ui-autocomplete-input"
autocomplete="off" role="textbox" aria-
```

```
autocomplete="list" aria-haspopup="true">
</textarea>
</body>
  </html>
```

<fieldset>

Used to create a group of related elements on a form and creates a box over the elements. The <legend> tag is used to define the name of the child content. Legend elements are the parent element and define a label for the <fieldset> element.

Syntax:

```
<fieldset> … </fieldset>
```

Example:

```
<!DOCTYPE html>
<html>
<head>
  <style>
   fieldset{
    background-color: burlywood;
    }
  </style>
<body>
  <form>

    <fieldset>
        <legend>Details</legend>
        Name: <input type = "text" name = "Name">
<br />
        Subjects:<input type = "text" name =
"Subjects"> <br />
       Age :<input type = "number" name = "Age">
    </fieldset>

  </form>
</body>
  </html>
```

<legend>

This acts as a caption for the <fieldset> element. The <label> element defines a label for several form elements.

Syntax:

```
<legend> ... </legend>
```

Example:

```
<!DOCTYPE html>
<html>
<head>
  <style>
   legend{
    background-color: burlywood;
   }
  </style>
<body>
  <form>

    <fieldset>
       <legend>Details</legend>
         Name: <input type = "text" name = "Name">
<br />
         Subjects:<input type = "text" name =
"Subjects"> <br />
       Age :<input type = "number" name = "Age">
    </fieldset>

  </form>
</body>
  </html>
```

<select>

The <select> element defines a control that provides a menu of options to choose from.

Syntax:

```
<select>... </select>
```

Example:

```html
<!DOCTYPE html>
<html>
<head>
  <style>
   :root {
   --gray: #34495e;
   --darkgray: #2c3e50;
}

select {
  /* Reset Select */
  appearance: none;
  outline: 0;
  border: 0;
  box-shadow: none;
  /* Personalize */
  flex: 1;
  padding: 0 1em;
  color: #fff;
  background-color: var(--darkgray);
  background-image: none;
  cursor: pointer;
}
/* Remove IE arrow */
select::-ms-expand {
  display: none;
}
/* Custom Select wrapper */
.select {
  position: relative;
  display: flex;
  width: 20em;
  height: 3em;
  border-radius: .25em;
  overflow: hidden;
}
/* Arrow */
.select::after {
  content: '\25BC';
  position: absolute;
  top: 0;
  right: 0;
```

```
    padding: 1em;
    background-color: #34495e;
    transition:. 25s all ease;
    pointer-events: none;
}
/* Transition */
.select:hover::after {
    color: #f39c12;
}

/* Other styles*/
body {
    color: #fff;
    background: var(--background-gradient);
}
h1 {
    margin: 0 0 0.25em;
}
a {
    font-weight: bold;
    color: var(--gray);
    text-decoration: none;
    padding: .25em;
    border-radius: .25em;
    background: white;
}

    </style>
  <body>
    <div class="select">
      <select>
        <option value="1">Select Option </option>
        <option value="2"> HTML </option>
        <option value="3"> CSS </option>
      </select>
    </div>

  </body>
    </html>
```

<option>...</option>

The <option> tag is an option in a picklist. <option> elements are part of <select>, <optgroup>, or <datalist> elements.

Here are some attributes of <option> tags:

- value="": The text is visible to the user for given option.

- Selected: It determines which option is selected by default when the form loads.

<optgroup>

The <optgroup> HTML element is used to create a grouping of options within a <select> element.

Syntax:

```
<optgroup> ... </optgroup>
```

Example:

```
<!DOCTYPE html>
<html>
<head>
  <style>

  </style>
<body>
  <select>
    <option value="">-- Select Language --
</option>
    <optgroup label=" Front end Language ">
      <option value="html"> HTML </option>
      <option value="css"> CSS </option>
      <option value="javascript"> Javascript
</option>
    </optgroup>
    <optgroup label="Back end Language">
      <option value="django"> Django </option>
      <option value="php"> PHP </option>
    </optgroup>
  </select>
</body>
  </html>
```

<progress> ... </progress>

The <progress> element displays an indicator showing the progress of a task, usually displayed in the form of a progress bar.

<datalist>...</datalist>

The <datalist> HTML element is used to provide predefined options for the <input> element. It adds an auto-fill feature to it.

<button>...</button>

The <button> element represents a clickable button that can be used on forms or anywhere standard button functionality is needed in an HTML document.

FORM ATTRIBUTES EVENTS LIST

Events triggered by actions inside an HTML form (applies to almost all HTML elements, but is mostly used in form elements):

- onblur: It fires the moment that the element loses focus.

- onchange: It fires the moment when the value of the element is changed.

- oncontextmenu: It is a script to be run when a context menu is triggered.

- onfocus: It fires the moment when the element gets focused.

- oninput: It is a script to be run when an element gets user input.

- oninvalid: It is a script to be run when an element is invalid.

- onreset: It fires when the Reset button in a form is clicked.

- onsearch: It fires when the user writes something in a search field (for <input="search">).

- onselect: It fires after some text has been selected in an element.

- onsubmit: It fires when a form is submitted.

KEYBOARD ATTRIBUTES EVENTS LIST

- onkeydown: It fires when a user is pressing a key.

- onkeypress: It fires when a user presses a key.

- onkeyup: It fires when a user releases a key.

MOUSE ATTRIBUTES EVENTS LIST

- onclick: It fires on a mouse click on the element.

- ondblclick: It fires on a mouse double-click on the element.

- onmousedown: It fires when a mouse button is pressed down on an element.

- onmousemove: It fires when the mouse pointer is moving while it is over an element.

- onmouseout: It fires when the mouse pointer moves out of an element.

- onmouseover: It fires when the mouse pointer moves over an element.

- onmouseup: It fires when a mouse button is released over an element.

- onmousewheel: Now, it is deprecated but use the onwheel attribute instead.

- onwheel: It fires when the mouse wheel rolls up or down over an element.

DRAG ATTRIBUTES EVENTS LIST

- ondrag: It is a script to be run when an element is dragged.

- ondragend: It is a script to be run at the end of a drag operation.

- ondragenter: It is a script to be run when an element has been dragged to a valid drop target.

- ondragleave: It is a script to be run when an element leaves a valid drop target.

- ondragover: It is a script to be run when an element is being dragged over a valid drop target.

- ondragstart: It is a script to be run at the start of a drag operation.

- ondrop: It is a script to be run when dragged element is being dropped.

- onscroll: It is a script to be run when an element's scrollbar is being scrolled.

WINDOW ATTRIBUTES EVENTS LIST

The events related to the window object:

- onafterprint: It fires after the associated document is printed.

- onbeforeprint: It fires before the associated document is printed.

- onbeforeunload: It fires before a document is unloaded.

- onerror: It fires when document errors occur.

- onhashchange: It fires when the fragment identifier part of the document's URL, i.e. the small portion of a URL follows the sign (#) changes.

- onload: It fires when the document has finished loading.

- onmessage: It fires when the message event occurs, i.e. when user sends a cross-document message or a message is sent from a client with postMessage() method.

- onoffline: It fires when the network connection fails and the browser starts working offline.

- ononline: It fires when the network connections return and the browser starts working online.

- onpagehide: It fires when the page is hidden, such as when a user is moving to another web page.

- onpageshow: It fires when the page is shown, such as when a user navigates to a web page.

- onpopstate: It fires when changes are made to the active history.

- onresize: It fires when the browser window is resized.

- onstorage: It fires when a Web Storage area is updated.

- onunload: It fires immediately before the document is unloaded or the browser window is closed.

MEDIA ATTRIBUTES EVENTS LIST

Events that occur when handling media elements that are embedded inside the documents, such as <audio> and <video> elements:

- onabort: It fires when playback is aborted, but not due to an error.

- oncanplay script: It fires when enough data is available to play the media, but would require further buffering.

- oncanplaythrough: It fires when entire media can be played to the end without requiring to stop for further buffering.

- oncuechange: It fires when the text track cue in a <track> element changes.

- ondurationchange: It fires when the duration of the media changes.

- onemptied: It fires when the media element is reset to its initial state, because of a fatal error during load, because the load() method is called to reload it.

- onended: It fires when the end of playback is reached.

- onerror: It fires when an error occurs while fetching the media data.

- onloadeddata: It fires when media data is loaded at the current playback position.

- onloadedmetadata: It fires when metadata of the media (like duration and dimensions) has finished loading.

- onloadstart: It fires when loading of the media begins.

- onpause: It fires when playback is paused, either by the user or programmatically.

- onplay: It fires when playback of the media starts after having been paused, i.e. when the play() method is requested.

- Playing: It fires when the audio or video has started playing.

- Progress: It fires periodically to indicate the progress while downloading the media data.

- onratechange: It fires when the playback rate or speed is increased or decreased, like slow motion or fast forward mode.

- Onseeked: It fires when the seek operation ends.

- Seeking: It fires when the current playback position is moved.

- installed: It fires when the download has stopped unexpectedly.

- Unsuspend: It fires when the loading of the media is intentionally stopped.

- ontimeupdate: It fires when the playback position changes, like when the user fast-forwards to a different playback position.

- Onvolumechange: It fires when the volume is changed, or playback is muted or unmuted.

- Onwaiting: It fires when playback stops because the next frame of a video resource is not available.

HTML TABLES

HTML tables allow the developers to organize data into rows and columns. HTML tables allow web authors to organize data such as text, images, links, other tables, etc. into rows and columns of cells. HTML tables are created by the <table> tag, where the <tr> tag is used to create table rows and the <td> tag is used to create data cells. Elements below <td> are normal and left-aligned by default.

<table> ... </table>

It marks a table in a web page and represents data in a two-dimensional table comprised of rows and columns.

Example:

```
<!DOCTYPE html>
<html>
<head>
<style>
table {
   font-family: Arial, sans-serif;
   border-collapse: collapse;
```

```
    width: 100%;
  }

Ltd, the {
  border: 1px solid #dddddd;
  text-align: left;
  padding: 8px;
}

tr:nth-child(even) {
  background-color: #dddddd;
}
</style>
</head>
<body>

<h2>HTML Table</h2>

<table>
  <tr>
    <th> Name </th>
    <th> Age </th>
    <th> Class </th>
  </tr>
  <tr>
    <td> Kiran </td>
    <td> 21 </td>
    <td> 6th </td>
  </tr>
  <tr>
    <td> Soni </td>
    <td> 22 </td>
    <td> 7th </td>
  </tr>
  <tr>
    <td> Jot </td>
    <td> 20 </td>
    <td> 8th </td>
  </tr>
</table>

</body>
</html>
```

<caption> ... </caption>

Description of the table is placed inside this tag and it specifies the title or caption of a table.

```
<!DOCTYPE html>
<html>
<head>
<style>
table {
  font-family: Arial, sans-serif;
  border-collapse: collapse;
  width: 100%;
}

Ltd, the {
  border: 1px solid #dddddd;
  text-align: left;
  padding: 8px;
}

tr:nth-child(even) {
  background-color: #dddddd;
}
caption{
  font-size:28px;
  color: blue;
}
h2{
  text-align: center;
}
</style>
</head>
<body>

<h2>HTML Table</h2>

<table>
  <caption> User Information Table</caption>
  <tr>
    <th> Name </th>
    <th> Age </th>
    <th> Class </th>
  </tr>
```

```
<tr>
   <td> Kiran </td>
   <td> 21 </td>
   <td> 6th </td>
</tr>
<tr>
   <td> Soni </td>
   <td> 22 </td>
   <td> 7th </td>
</tr>
<tr>
   <td> Jot </td>
   <td> 20 </td>
   <td> 8th </td>
</tr>
</table>

</body>
</html>
```

<thead> ... </thead>

It specifies information pertaining to specific columns of the table. It is used to group header content in an HTML table.

<tbody> ... </tbody>

The body of a table, where the data is held. It is used to group the primary content of an HTML table.

Example:

```
<!DOCTYPE html>
<html>
<head>
<!DOCTYPE html>
<html>
<head>
<style>
body{
   padding:10px;
   width:400px;
   margin:0 auto;
}
```

```
h1{
  text-align: center;
}
table {
  font-family: Arial, sans-serif;
  border-collapse: collapse;
  width: 100%;
}

Ltd, the {
  border: 1px solid #dddddd;
  text-align: left;
  padding: 8px;
}
tbody{
  background-color: lightslategray;
}
</style>

</head>
<body>
  <table>
    <caption> User Information Table</caption>
    <thead>
      <th> Name </th>
      <th> Age </th>
      <th> Class </th>
    </thead>

  <tbody>
    <tr>
      <td> Kiran </td>
      <td> 21 </td>
      <td> 6th </td>
    </tr>
    <tr>
      <td> Soni </td>
      <td> 22 </td>
      <td> 7th </td>
    </tr>
    <tr>
      <td> Jot </td>
      <td> 20 </td>
```

```
          <td> 8th </td>
        </tr>
      </tbody>

      <tfoot>
        <tr>
          <td> Jot </td>
          <td> 20 </td>
          <td> 8th </td>
        </tr>
      </tfoot>
      </table>

        </body>
      </html>
```

<tfoot> ... </tfoot>

It determines the footer of the table and defines a set of rows summarizing the columns of the table as per requirement.

Example:

```
<!DOCTYPE html>
<html>
<head>
<!DOCTYPE html>
<html>
<head>
<style>
body{
  padding:10px;
  width:400px;
  margin:0 auto;
}
h1{
  text-align: center;
}
table {
  font-family: Arial, sans-serif;
  border-collapse: collapse;
  width: 100%;
}
```

```
Ltd, the {
  border: 1px solid #dddddd;
  text-align: left;
  padding: 8px;
}
tfoot{
  background-color: lightslategray;
}
</style>

</head>
<body>
  <table>
    <caption> User Information Table</caption>
    <thead>
      <th> Name </th>
      <th> Age </th>
      <th> Class </th>
    </thead>

  <tbody>
    <tr>
      <td> Kiran </td>
      <td> 21 </td>
      <td> 6th </td>
    </tr>
    <tr>
      <td> Soni </td>
      <td> 22 </td>
      <td> 7th </td>
    </tr>
    <tr>
      <td> Jot </td>
      <td> 20 </td>
      <td> 8th </td>
    </tr>
  </tbody>

  <tfoot>
    <tr>
      <td> Jot </td>
      <td> 20 </td>
```

```
      <td> 8th </td>
    </tr>
  </tfoot>
  </table>

  </body>
</html>
```

<tr> ... </tr>

It denotes a single row in a table. It defines a row in an HTML table. A <tr>
element contains one or more <th> or <td> elements.

```
<!DOCTYPE html>
<html>
<head>
<!DOCTYPE html>
<html>
<head>
<style>
body{
  padding:10px;
  width:400px;
  margin:0 auto;
}
h1{
  text-align: center;
}
table {
  font-family: Arial, sans-serif;
  border-collapse: collapse;
  width: 100%;
}

Ltd, the {
  border: 1px solid #dddddd;
  text-align: left;
  padding: 8px;
}

tr:nth-child(even) {
  background-color: yellow;
}
```

```
tr:nth-child(odd) {
  background-color: greenyellow;
}
</style>

</head>
<body>
  <table>
    <caption> User Information Table</caption>
    <tr>
      <th> Name </th>
      <th> Age </th>
      <th> Class </th>
    </tr>
    <tr>
      <td> Kiran </td>
      <td> 21 </td>
      <td> 6th </td>
    </tr>
    <tr>
      <td> Soni </td>
      <td> 22 </td>
      <td> 7th </td>
    </tr>
    <tr>
      <td> Jot </td>
      <td> 20 </td>
      <td> 8th </td>
    </tr>
  </table>
    </body>
  </html>
```

<th> ... </th>

The value of a heading of a table's column is used to define a cell as the header of a group of cells of the HTML table.

Example:

```
<!DOCTYPE html>
<html>
<head>
<!DOCTYPE html>
```

```html
<html>
<head>
<style>
body{
  padding:10px;
  width:400px;
  margin:0 auto;
}
h1{
  text-align: center;
}
table {
  font-family: Arial, sans-serif;
  border-collapse: collapse;
  width: 100%;
}

Ltd, the {
  border: 1px solid #dddddd;
  text-align: left;
  padding: 8px;
}

th:nth-child(even) {
  background-color: yellow;
}
th:nth-child(odd) {
  background-color: greenyellow;
}
</style>

</head>
<body>
  <table>
    <caption> User Information Table</caption>
    <tr>
      <th> Name </th>
      <th> Age </th>
      <th> Class </th>
    </tr>
    <tr>
      <td> Kiran </td>
      <td> 21 </td>
```

```
      <td> 6th </td>
    </tr>
    <tr>
      <td> Soni </td>
      <td> 22 </td>
      <td> 7th </td>
    </tr>
    <tr>
      <td> Jot </td>
      <td> 20 </td>
      <td> 8th </td>
    </tr>
  </table>

  </body>
</html>
```

<td> ... </td>

A single cell of a table. It contains the actual value/data that defines a cell of a table that contains the main data of the table.

Example:

```
<!DOCTYPE html>
<html>
<head>
<!DOCTYPE html>
<html>
<head>
<style>
body{
   padding:10px;
   width:400px;
   margin:0 auto;
}
h1{
   text-align: center;
}
table {
   font-family: Arial, sans-serif;
   border-collapse: collapse;
   width: 100%;
}
```

```
Ltd, the {
  border: 1px solid #dddddd;
  text-align: left;
  padding: 8px;
}

td:nth-child(even) {
  background-color: yellow;
}
td:nth-child(odd) {
  background-color: greenyellow;
}
</style>

</head>
<body>
  <table>
    <caption> User Information Table</caption>
    <tr>
      <th> Name </th>
      <th> Age </th>
      <th> Class </th>
    </tr>
    <tr>
      <td> Kiran </td>
      <td> 21 </td>
      <td> 6th </td>
    </tr>
    <tr>
      <td> Soni </td>
      <td> 22 </td>
      <td> 7th </td>
    </tr>
    <tr>
      <td> Jot </td>
      <td> 20 </td>
      <td> 8th </td>
    </tr>
  </table>

    </body>
  </html>
```

<colgroup> ... </colgroup>

Used for grouping columns together. It represents a group of one or more columns within a table in a document. It can be used to style across one or more columns.

Example:

```
<!DOCTYPE html>
<html>
<head>
<!DOCTYPE html>
<html>
<head>
<style>
body{
  padding:10px;
  width:400px;
  margin:0 auto;
}
h1{
  text-align: center;
}
table {
  font-family: Arial, sans-serif;
  border-collapse: collapse;
  width: 100%;
}

Ltd, the {
  border: 1px solid #dddddd;
  text-align: left;
  padding: 8px;
}
colgroup{
  background-color: lightslategray;
}
.total {
 background-color: #eeeeee;
}
```

```
</style>
<table>
<colgroup>
 <col span="3">
 <col class="total">
</colgroup>
<tr>
<th> Item </th>
<th> Qty. </th>
<th> Price </th>
<th> Cost </th>
</tr>
<tr>
<tr>
<td> Bananas </td>
<td> 5 </td>
<td> 0.50 </td>
<td> 2.50 </td>
</tr>
<tr>
<td> Apples </td>
<td> 2 </td>
<td> 0.25 </td>
<td> 0.50 </td>
</tr>
<tr>
<td> Oranges </td>
<td> 3 </td>
<td> 0.75 </td>
<td> 2.25 </td>
</tr>
<tr>
<td colspan="3"> TOTAL </td>
<td> 5.25 </td>
</tr>
</table>

   </body>
  </html>
```

<col>

It denotes a column inside a table. To apply different properties to a column within a colgroup, you can use the <col> tag within the <colgroup> tag.

HTML MULTIMEDIA

You can hear or see multimedia in the form of images. It comes in different formats. HTML helps you add multimedia files to a website by providing various multimedia tags.

<img>

The <img> tag is used to link images to web pages. <img />

Example:

```
<!DOCTYPE html>
<html>
<head>

</head>
<body>
<img src="https://images.pexels.com/
photos/13076228/pexels-photo-13076228.jpeg?auto=co
mpress&cs=tinysrgb&w=400&lazy=load" alt="wall
flower" height="200px" width="300px">
</body>
</html>
```

<audio>

The <audio> HTML element is used to include audio content in documents. It can contain one or more audio sources.

Syntax:

```
<audio>...</audio>
```

Example:

```
<!DOCTYPE html>
```

```html
<html>
<head>
<title> HTML </title>
</head>
<body>
  <audio controls>
    <source src="song.mp3" type="audio/mp3">
  </audio>
</body>
</html>
```

\<video\>

The \<video\> element embeds a media player that supports video files document.

Syntax:

```html
<video>...</video>
```

Example:

```html
<!DOCTYPE html>
<html>
<head>
<title> HTML </title>
</head>
<body>
  <video width="320" height="240" controls>
    <source src="https://www.youtube.com/
watch?v=WVEcnIBh5kY" type="video/mp4">
    Your browser doesn't support the video tag.
  </video>
</body>
</html>
```

\<figure\>

The \<figure\> tag is used to group various diagrams, figures, illustrations, and code snippets into a document.

Syntax:

```html
<figure>...</figure>
```

Example:

```
<!DOCTYPE html>
<html>
<head>
<title> HTML </title>
</head>
<body>

  <figure>
    <img src="https://images.pexels.com/
photos/13554908/pexels-photo-13554908.jpeg?auto=co
mpress&cs=tinysrgb&w=400&lazy=load" alt="flower"
height="300px" width="200px">
    <figcaption>Fig.1 - Flower </figcaption>
  </figure>
</body>
</html>
```

<figcaption>

The HTML tag <figcaption> is used inside the <figure> tag to describe the content.

Syntax:

```
<figcaption>…</figcaption>

<!DOCTYPE html>
<html>
<head>
<title> HTML </title>
</head>
<body>

  <figure>
    <img src="https://images.pexels.com/
photos/13554908/pexels-photo-13554908.jpeg?auto=comp
ress&cs=tinysrgb&w=400&lazy=load" alt="flower"
height="300px" width="200px">
    <figcaption> Fig.1 - Flower </figcaption>
  </figure>
</body>
</html>
```

<embed>

The <embed> tag helps embed multimedia into a web page and plays it when the page is opened. It uses three mandatory attributes namely src, height, and width.

Syntax:

```
<embed>...</embed>
```

Example:

```
<!DOCTYPE html>
<html>
<head>
<title> HTML </title>
</head>
<body>

  <embed type="image/jpg" src="https://images.
pexels.com/photos/13554908/pexels-photo-13554908.
jpeg?auto=compress&cs=tinysrgb&w=400&lazy=load"
width="300" height="200">

</body>
</html>
```

<object>

The <object> tag is used to add objects such as images, audio, video, Applets, ActiveX, Portable Document Format (PDF), and Flash objects on a web page.

Syntax:

```
<object>...</object>
```

Example:

```
<!DOCTYPE html>
<html>
<head>
<title> HTML </title>
</head>
```

```
<body>
    <object data="https://images.pexels.com/
photos/13554908/pexels-photo-13554908.jpeg?auto=co
mpress&cs=tinysrgb&w=400&lazy=load" width="300"
height="200"></object>
</body>
</html>
```

HTML CHARACTERS AND SYMBOLS

Some characters are reserved in HTML and have special meanings when used in HTML documents. HTML provides a wide variety of characters and symbols, including arrows, currency, letters, math, punctuation, and symbols. Some of the most commonly used are:

HTML CHARACTER ENTITIES

Here is the complete list of the character entity references. The following table lists the essential entities in HTML.

Character	Entity Name	Entity Number	Description
&	&amp;	&#38;	Ampersand
"	&quot;	&#34;	Double quote mark
<	&lt;	&#60;	Less than symbol
>	&gt;	&#62;	Greater than symbol
'	&apos;	&#39;	Apostrophe (XHTML in only)

COPYRIGHT, TRADEMARK, AND REGISTERED SYMBOL

The following lists the entities for copyright, trademark, and registered symbol.

Character	Name	Number	Description
©	&copy;	&#169;	Copyright
®	&reg;	&#174;	Registered
™	&trade;	&#8482;	Trademark

PUNCTUATION SYMBOL

The following lists the entities for general punctuation.

Character	Name	Number	Description
			It is En space
			It is Em space

(Continued)

Character	Name	Number	Description
			It is Thin space
			It is Nonbreaking space
–	&ndash;	&#8211;	It is En dash
—	&mdash;	&#8212;	It is Em dash
'	&lsquo;	&#8216;	It is Left/Opening single-quote
'	&rsquo;	&#8217;	It is Right/Closing single-quote and apostrophe
‚	&sbquo;	&#8218;	It is Single low-9 quotation mark
"	&ldquo;	&#8220;	It is Left/Opening double-quote
"	&rdquo;	&#8221;	It is Right/Closing double-quote
„	&bdquo;	&#8222;	It is Double low-9 quotation mark
‹	&lsaquo;	&#8249;	Left-pointing single-angle quotation mark
›	&rsaquo;	&#8250;	Left-pointing single-angle quotation mark
«	&laquo;	&#171;	Left-pointing double-angle quotation mark
«	&laquo;	&#171;	Left-pointing double-angle quotation mark
»	&raquo;	&#187;	Right-pointing double-angle quotation mark
†	&dagger;	&#8224;	Dagger
‡	&Dagger;	&#8224;	Double dagger
•	&bull;	&#8226;	Bullet
…	&hellep;	&#8230;	Ellipses
‰	&permil;	&#8240;	Per mille symbol (per thousand)
′	&prime;	&#8242;	Prime, minutes, feet
″	&Prime;	&#8243;	Double prime, seconds, inches
‾	&oline;	&#8254;	Overline
/	&frasl;	&#8260;	Fraction slash

ARROWS SYMBOL

The following lists the entities for arrows.

Character	Name	Entity	Explanation
←	&larr;	&#8592;	It is Left arrow
↑	&uarr;	&#8593;	It is Up arrow
→	&rarr;	&#8594;	It is Right arrow
↓	&darr;	&#8595;	It is Down arrow
↔	&harr;	&#8596;	It is Left-right arrow
↵	&crarr;	&#8629;	It is Down arrow with corner leftward
⇐	&lArr;	&#8656;	It is Leftward double arrow
⇑	&uArr;	&#8657;	It is Upward double arrow
⇒	&rArr;	&#8658;	It is Rightward double arrow
⇓	&dArr;	&#8659;	It is Downward double arrow
⇔	&hArr;	&#8660;	It is Left-right double arrow

MATHEMATICAL SYMBOLS

The following lists the entities for mathematical symbols.

Character	Name	Number	Description
∀	&forall;	&#8704;	It is for all
∂	&part;	&#8706;	It is Partial differential
∃	&exist;	&#8707;	It is there exists
∅	&empty;	&#8709;	Empty set, null set, diameter
∇	&nabla;	&#8711;	Nabla, backward difference
∈	&isin;	&#8712;	Element of
∉	&notin;	&#8713;	Not an element of
∋	&ni;	&#8715;	Contains as a member
∏	&prod;	&#8719;	N-ary product, product sign
∑	&sum;	&#8721;	N-ary summation
−	&minus;	&#8722;	Minus sign
∗	&lowast;	&#8727;	Asterisk operator
√	&radic;	&#8730;	Square root, radical sign
∝	&prop;	&#8733;	Proportional to
∞	&infin;	&#8734;	Infinity
∠	&ang;	&#8736;	Angle
∧	&and;	&#8743;	Logical and wedge
∨	&or;	&#8744;	Logical or, vee
∩	&cap;	&#8745;	Intersection, cap
∪	&cup;	&#8746;	Union, cup
∫	&int;	&#8747;	Integral
∴	&there4;	&#8756;	Therefore
~	&sim;	&#8764;	Tilde operator, varies with, similar to
≅	&cong;	&#8773;	Approximately equal to
≈	&asymp;	&#8776;	Almost equal to, asymptotic to
≠	&ne;	&#8800;	Not equal to
≡	&equiv;	&#8801;	Equivalent to
≤	&le;	&#8804;	Less than or equal to
≥	&ge;	&#8805;	Greater than or equal to
⊂	&sub;	&#8834;	Subset of
⊃	&sup;	&#8835;	Superset of
⊄	&nsub;	&#8836;	Not a subset of
⊆	&sube;	&#8838;	Subset of or equal to
⊇	&supe;	&#8839;	Superset of or equal to
⊕	&oplus;	&#8853;	Circled plus, direct sum
⊗	&otimes;	&#8855;	Circled times, vector product
⊥	&perp;	&#8869;	It is Up tack, orthogonal to, perpendicular
·	&sdot;	&#8901;	It is Dot operator

OTHER SYMBOL

The following lists the other entities supported by HTML language.

Character	Name	Number	Description
⌈	&lceil;	&#8968;	It is Left ceiling
⌉	&rceil;	&#8969;	It is Right ceiling
⌊	&lfloor;	&#8970;	It is Left floor
⌋	&rfloor;	&#8971;	It is Right floor
⟨	&lang;	&#10216;	It is Left-pointing angle bracket
⟩	&rang;	&#10217;	It is Right-pointing angle bracket
◊	&loz;	&#9674;	It is Lozenge
ℑ	&image;	&#8465;	It is Blackletter capital I, imaginary part
℘	&weierp;	&#8472;	It is Script capital P, power set
ℜ	&real;	&#8476;	It is Blackletter capital R, real part
ℵ	&alefsym;	&#8501;	It is Alef symbol, or first transfinite cardinal
♠	&spades;	&#9824;	It is Black spade suit
♣	&clubs;	&#9827;	It is Black club suit
♥	&hearts;	&#9829;	It is Blackheart suit
♦	&diams;	&#9830;	It is Black diamond suit

CURRENCY SYMBOLS

The following lists the entities for currency symbols.

Character	Name	Number	Description
¢	&cent;	&#162;	It is Cent
£	&pound;	&#163;	It is Pound
¤	&curren;	&#164;	It is General currency
¥	&yen;	&#165;	It is Yen
€	&euro;	&#8364;	It is Euro

HTML ATTRIBUTES

HTML attributes are special words used to define the characteristics of an HTML element. These are modifiers placed inside the opening tag of an element. Attributes have two parts – a name and a value. The name is the property you want to set and the value is the required value of the attribute.

alt: The alt attribute is used with an image tag. It helps us specify alternative text in case the image cannot be displayed on the site so that users can have an idea of what the image contains. < tag_name ="”…” >

Example:

```
<!DOCTYPE html>
<html>
  <head>
  <title> HTML </title>
  </head>
  <body>
    <img src="flower.jpg" alt=" A pink flower"
width="500" height="600">
</html>
```

href: We use the <a> tag to describe a hyperlink. The href attribute specifies the destination URL. Without the href <a> attribute, the element will not become a hyperlink. < tag_name ="…" >.

The href attribute can be used on the following elements:

- <a>

- <area>

- <base>

- <link>

Example:

```
<!DOCTYPE html>
<html>
  <head>
<title> HTML </title>
<base href="https://www.google.com/"
target="_blank">
<link rel="stylesheet" href="styles.css">
  </head>
  <body>
    <a href="https://www.google.com"> Google </a>

    <img src="an_image.jpg" alt="Workplace"
usemap="#workmap" width="400" height="379">

<map name="workmap">
  <area shape="name_of_shape"
coords="34,44,270,350" alt="name of shape"
href="name_of_shape.htm">
```

```
   <area shape="name_of_shape"
coords="290,172,333,250" alt="name of shape"
href="name_of_shape.htm">
   <area shape="name_of_shape" coords="337,300,44"
alt="name of shape" href="name_of_shape.htm">
</map>
     </body>
</html>
```

src: The src attribute is used to define the URL of the image to be used as the submit button. It specifies the image path inside the double quotes. < tag_name ="..." >

The attribute can be used on the following elements:

- <script>

- <src>

Example:

```
<!DOCTYPE html>
<html>
   <head>
<title> HTML </title>
<base href="https://www.google.com/"
target="_blank">
<link rel="stylesheet" href="styles.css">
   </head>
   <body>

     <a href="https://www.google.com"> Google </a>

   <img src="an_image.jpg" alt="an_image" >
     </body>
<script src="script.js" type=" text/javascript" >
</script>

</html>
```

width: The tag also contains a width attribute. As the name suggests, these attributes determine the width of the image in pixels). < tag_name ="..." >. The width attribute can be used with the following elements such as:

- <canvas>

- <embed>

- <iframe>

- <img>

- <input>

- <object>

- <video>

Example:

```
<!DOCTYPE html>
<html>
  <head>
<title> HTML </title>
<base href="https://www.google.com/"
target="_blank">
<link rel="stylesheet" href="styles.css">
  </head>
  <body>
    <canvas id="myCanvas" width="200" height="200"
style="border:1px solid">
      Your browser does not support the HTML5
canvas tag.
    </canvas>
    <embed type="image/jpg" src="https://images.
pexels.com/photos/13234870/pexels-photo-13234870.
jpeg?auto=compress&cs=tinysrgb&w=400&lazy=load"
width="200" height="300">

      <iframe src="https://www.google.com/"
width="450" height="200"> </iframe>

      <img src="https://images.pexels.com/
photos/13234870/pexels-photo-13234870.jpeg?auto=co
mpress&cs=tinysrgb&w=400&lazy=load" alt="Smiley
face" height="250" width="250">

      <form action="/action_page.php">
```

```
    Image type: <input type="image"
src="https://images.pexels.com/photos/13234870/
pexels-photo-13234870.jpeg?auto=compress&cs=tinysr
gb&w=400&lazy=load" alt="Submit" width="250"
height="250">
    </form>

    <object data="https://images.pexels.com/
photos/13234870/pexels-photo-13234870.jpeg?auto=co
mpress&cs=tinysrgb&w=400&lazy=load" width="300"
height="200"></object>

    <video width="320" height="240" controls>
      <source src="https://www.youtube.com/
watch?v=WVEcnIBh5kY" type="video/mp4">
      Your browser doesn't support the video tag.
    </video>

  <script>
    var c = document.getElementById("myCanvas");
    var ctx = c.getContext("2d");
    ctx.fillStyle = "#92B";
    ctx.fillRect(40, 40, 90, 90);
  </script>
</body>
</html>
```

height: The tag also contains a height attribute. As the name suggests, these attributes determine the height of the image in pixels). < tag_name ="..." >. The width attribute can be used on the following elements such as:

- <canvas>
- <embed>
- <iframe>
- <img>
- <input>
- <object>
- <video>

Example:

```html
<!DOCTYPE html>
<html>
  <head>
<title> HTML </title>
<base href="https://www.google.com/"
target="_blank">
<link rel="stylesheet" href="styles.css">
  </head>
  <body>
    <canvas id="myCanvas" width="200" height="200"
style="border:1px solid">
      Your browser does not support the HTML5
canvas tag.
    </canvas>
    <embed type="image/jpg" src="https://images.
pexels.com/photos/13234870/pexels-photo-13234870.
jpeg?auto=compress&cs=tinysrgb&w=400&lazy=load"
width="200" height="300">

      <iframe src="https://www.google.com/"
width="450" height="200"> </iframe>

      <img src="https://images.pexels.com/
photos/13234870/pexels-photo-13234870.jpeg?auto=co
mpress&cs=tinysrgb&w=400&lazy=load" alt="Smiley
face" height="250" width="250">

      <form action="/action_page.php">
       Image type: <input type="image"
src="https://images.pexels.com/photos/13234870/
pexels-photo-13234870.jpeg?auto=compress&cs=tinysr
gb&w=400&lazy=load" alt="Submit" width="250"
height="250">
      </form>

      <object data="https://images.pexels.com/
photos/13234870/pexels-photo-13234870.jpeg?auto=co
mpress&cs=tinysrgb&w=400&lazy=load" width="300"
height="200"></object>

      <video width="320" height="240" controls>
```

```
        <source src="https://www.youtube.com/
watch?v=WVEcnIBh5kY" type="video/mp4">
        Your browser doesn't support the video tag.
    </video>

    <script>
      var c = document.getElementById("myCanvas");
      var ctx = c.getContext("2d");
      ctx.fillStyle = "#92B";
      ctx.fillRect(40, 40, 90, 90);
    </script>
</body>
</html>
```

style: The style attribute helps us to change the look and feel of a document by setting the style like font, size, color, etc. of an HTML element. < tag_name ="..." >

Example:

```
<!DOCTYPE html>
<html>
  <head>
<title> HTML </title>
<base href="https://www.google.com/"
target="_blank">
<link rel="stylesheet" href="styles.css">
  </head>
  <body>
    <h1 style="color: blue; text-align:
center">This is a header</h1>
    <p style="color:green;font-size:28px">This is
a paragraph.</p>
</body>
</html>
```

id: This id attribute is a unique identifier used to identify an area of a web page. It uses CSS and JavaScript to perform a specific task for a unique element. The id attribute is using the # symbol followed by id. < tag_name ="..." >

Example:

```
<!DOCTYPE html>
<html>
  <head>
<title> HTML </title>
<base href="https://www.google.com/"
target="_blank">
<link rel="stylesheet" href="styles.css">
  </head>
  <body>
    <p>  You are learning </p><h1
id="myHeader">  </h1>
    <button onclick="result()">Change text</button>

    <script>
      function result() {
        document.getElementById("myHeader").
innerHTML = " HTML ";
      }
      </script>

</body>
</html>
```

class: The class attribute is used to define one or more class names for an element and to assign different properties within a single block, which in turn can be assigned to any element. Once assigned a specific class, elements will have all the properties of that specific class. < tag_name ="..." >

Example:

```
<!DOCTYPE html>
<html>
  <head>
<title> HTML </title>
<style>
 .myHeader{
    font-size: 20px;
    color:blue;
  }
```

```
</style>
  </head>
  <body>
    <p> You are learning </p><h1 class="myHeader">
HTML </h1>
</body>
</html>
```

title: The title attribute defines extra information about the element. In most browsers, the text of the title attribute is most often displayed as a hint when hovering over an element. < tag_name ="..." >

Example:

```
<!DOCTYPE html>
<html>
  <head>
<title> HTML </title>
  </head>
  <body>
    <p> <abbr title="Hyper Text Markup Language">
HTML </abbr> </p>
    <p title="Cascading Style Sheet"> CSS </p>
</body>
</html>
```

Placeholder: The placeholder attribute specifies a hint that describes the expected value of the input field/text area. Short help is displayed in the field before the user enters a value.

The placeholder attribute can be used on the following elements such as:

- <input>

- <textarea>

Example:

```
<!DOCTYPE html>
<html>
  <head>
```

```
<title> HTML </title>
  </head>
  <body>
    <form action="#">
      <label for="fname">First name:</label>
      <input type="text" id="fname" name="fname"
placeholder="First Name"> <br> <br>
      <label for="lname">Last name:</label>
      <input type="text" id="lname" name="lname"
placeholder="Last Name"> <br> <br>
      <input type="submit" value="Submit">
      <label for="phone">Enter a phone number:
</label> <br> <br>
    <input type="tel" id="phone" name="phone"
placeholder="123-45-678"> <br> <br>
    </form>
</body>
</html>
```

NEW HTML TAGS

In earlier articles, we saw the rise of HTML; they learned about the various elements and tags that make HTML awesome. In this section, we will understand the older problems solved by HTML5 and the new tags introduced with HTML5.

The HTML5 specification introduced a collection of new HTML tags that define semantic/structural elements, text formatting guidelines, form controls, input types, audio, video, and many other interesting elements. The section describes all of the new HTML5 tags along with updates to existing tags that take the capabilities of an HTML document to the next level.

HTML5 is the upgrade version of the previous version of HTML 4, which consists of a different set of new features, advanced functionality, better page display, and many other extensive improvements to meet the growing technological needs. It is based on the latest version of HTML5, the most used and requested elements such as <mark>, <article>, <header>, <figcaption>, <section>, <figure>, <main>, <footer>, < nav>, and elements <summary>. All these new HTML5 tags or DOM elements allow us to integrate a much better and more user-friendly interface along with higher performance, efficient results, easy configuration, and overall code implementation and finally, it allows us to have the best possible app development experience.

In HTML 4, semantic parts of a document were distinguished by different <div> elements. HTML5 solves this problem by introducing various new division elements such as <section>, <aside>, <article>, <header>, <footer>, etc. It makes the HTML5 outline algorithm to read the document more accurately and mark the path. Let's start with a list of the new HTML5 elements and their respective descriptions.

- <article>: It is a separate section that is used to include a blog, forum post, magazine article, etc. And to be more specific, the content in it is completely independent of the other child or the surrounding content of the web application.

- <aside>: It is used to include some information related to the main content. Essentially, this tag identifies content that is related to the primary content of the web page but does not account for the primary goal of the primary page request. The new <aside> tag mainly contains author information, links, related content, and other useful content.

- <bdi>: It is used to isolate enclosed text that may be formatted differently than text outside this tag.

- <details>: It creates an interactive section that displays its information when clicked.

- <dialog>: It is used to include a dialog box on a web page.

- <figcaption>: It is used to include a caption for a figure inside a <figure> element.

- <figure> Basically used to represent a figure and its label. This element is used to mark individual content like images, categorization, maps, code articles, and many other elements.

- <footer>: It is used to include footer content on a web page, such as license information, copyright information, etc.

- <header>: It is used to include header content on a web page, such as page information, summary, etc.

- <main>: It is used to include the main centralized theme of the web page.

- <mark>: It is used to highlight a piece of content on a web page.

- <meter>: It is used to include a scalar/fractional value within a specified range, not to be confused with the <progress> element.

- <nav>: It is used to provide navigational links such as menus.

- <progress>: It is used to include a progress bar on a web page. The progress bar value starts at 0 and goes to 100 as a number.

- <ruby>: It is used to include the ruby annotation. Example: Japanese characters.

- <rp>: It is used to enclose parentheses in a ruby character.

- <rt>: It is used to include the ruby annotation pronunciation.

- <section>: It is used to represent a section on a web page.

- <summary>: It is used to include information in the <details> element. Click on the <summary> element to display the information.

- <time>: It is used to include a Date/Time component in a web page.

- <wbr>: It is used to include a word break.

- <datalist>: Dropdown list, set of options.

- <output>: It is used to display the calculation result on a web page.

- <canvas>: It is used to draw animations and graphics on a web page. And it acts as a container for other graphic elements to be placed.

- <audio>: It is used to include audio content on a web page, such as playing songs or melodies.

- <embed>: It is used to include external plug-ins on a web page. In other words, the embedded element is used to embed external applications or iframe elements into an existing layout, which are generally multimedia content such as audio or video content as playback into an HTML document. Generally, the element is used as a wrapper or container to embed plug-ins such as flash animations and third-party videos via script.

- <source>: It is used to specify multiple media sources for <video>, <audio>, and <picture> elements.

- <track>: It is used within an <audio> or <video> element to handle titles, captions, descriptions, etc. of video or audio on a web page, in other words specifies tracks for audio and video elements.

- <video>: It is used to include video content on a web page.

NOTES

1. HTML Cheat Sheet – A Basic Guide to HTML – GeeksforGeeks. https://www.geeksforgeeks.org/html-cheat-sheet-a-basic-guide-to-html/, accessed on September 12, 2022.
2. The Complete HTML Cheat Sheet – https://www3.cs.stonybrook.edu/~pramod.ganapathi/doc/CSE102/CSE102-CheatSheetHTML.pdf, accessed on September 12, 2022.

Appraisal

This book represents the structure and content of HTML5. The book might be same as the others but it is an all-new concept. As compared to the other versions such as HTML 4, this edition focuses more on HTML5, which represents both a return to the markup past. However, we get some information from the previous version because we also focus on previous elements and not only on the future but also present all the elements supported in browsers today. With the help of this book we want to provide the reference you need in learning their syntax. However, in the case of web documents, the markup is in the form of traditional HTML and XML. The XML-focused variant, XHTML, is a bit more obvious. These are not very behind the scenes; markup languages are used to inform web browsers about the structure of a page and some can argue its presentation too.

Since its introduced in 1991, HTML (and later its XML-based cousin, XHTML) has gone through many changes. The first versions of HTML were used to compile the earliest websites that lacked a precise definition. Then Internet Engineering Task Force (IETF) began to standardize the language. In 1995, the first released HTML standard was in the form of HTML 2.0.

HTML is a markup language for creating web pages. Elements that are in the form of tags such as <em> and </em> are inserted into text documents to indicate to browsers how to render pages. Many of the elements that HTML5 adds that can be used immediately are semantic in nature. In this sense, HTML5 continues the appropriate goal of separating structure from style.

You can use lowercase, quote all attributes, and self-close empty elements it works well in HTML5 as well. However, HTML5 is not only about markup but also about metadata, media, Web applications, APIs, and more.

DOI: 10.1201/9781003357537-6

CAREER IN HTML

HTML developers or programmers should have a bachelor's degree in computer science. There are many platforms available for HTML developers to help them improve their HTML skills. With the help of HTML, anyone can create their own websites and websites for different suppliers.

Since HTML is mainly used with other scripting languages, the scope of HTML always remains in the top organization and will be used in any web development such as web pages and web applications, although it is useful for creating custom applications or web pages. HTML can be used in multiple languages and employers offer a good salary to web developers or HTML developers. HTML gives you customized features with less effort. A career in HTML is growing fast, and learns it for creating your own websites as well.

Web development has two main parts namely Front end and Back end. Front-end development is also called client-side web development. In this book, we have discussed front-end development in detail. This is mainly about creating websites or web applications for the client using HTML, CSS, and JavaScript. Anything that appears on the client side is something that users can interact with.

Front-end development is a constantly evolving field. Tools and techniques are constantly changing. A developer must always be ready to learn new skills because the market is very volatile. With every new library or framework that comes out, the developer has to constantly improve. Awareness of how the market is evolving is also important.

To become a front-end developer, one must learn how to architect and develop websites and applications using web technologies. These technologies run on an open web platform. They can also act as compilation input for non-web platforms such as React Native. Anyone entering the field of web development must learn HTML, CSS, and JavaScript. These three technologies are considered core.

HOW TO GET JOB AS FRONT-END WEB DEVELOPER AS WELL AS GAME DEVELOPER?

HTML is mainly required for front-end developers, full-stack developers, and UI/UX designers. It doesn't take long to learn HTML. Most new programmers can learn the basics of HTML in two to three weeks. However, daily practice is necessary to master the language and understand its full potential.

If you want to master the HTML, you should learn some topics of HTML such as:

- HTML structured

- HTML headings (<h1>, <h2>... <h6>)

- The <div> tag

- Presenting text using <p> and <span>

- Styling text using <style> and CSS

- Ordered and unordered lists (<ol> and <ul>)

- Adding image files (<img>)

- Table rows, columns, borders, head, body, and footer

- Form design and data collection

- Types of form questions like radio buttons, text boxes, and checkboxes

- CSS style rule

GAME DEVELOPMENT IN HTML5

HTML5 introduces many cutting-edge features such as 2D and 3D graphics, quality audio APIs, and offline asset storage that allow game developers to create immersive games. It enables the development of games that adapt to different resolutions, screen sizes, aspect ratios, and guidelines. HTML5 offers many JavaScript game engines and frameworks for developing 2D games, such as Contstruct2, Three.js, Play Canvas, Turbulenz, Kick.js., Minko, and Unity5. These game engines make it easy to develop 2D games. HTML5 allows access to all these technologies, unlike Flash.

HTML FEATURES

- HTML is the commonly used language for writing web pages.

- It is an easy-to-understand and editable language.

- You can do effective presentations that can be created using all its formatting tags.

- It provides a more flexible way to design web pages along with text.

- You can also add links to web pages so that readers can browse the information that interests them.

- HTML documents run on all platforms such as Macintosh, Windows, Linux, etc.

- More topics like graphics, videos, and sounds can also be added to the website to give your website an extra attractive look.

Index